A LIFE APART

A LIFE APART

*A pilot study of residential institutions
for the physically handicapped
and the young chronic sick*

E. J. MILLER & G. V. GWYNNE

TAVISTOCK PUBLICATIONS

First published in 1972
by Tavistock Publications Limited
11 New Fetter Lane, London EC4

First published as a Social Science Paperback in 1974
Reprinted 1974 and 1976

SBN 422 73910 3 (hardbound)
SBN 422 75660 1 (paperback)

This book is set in 11 pt Baskerville
and was printed in Great Britain
by William Clowes & Sons Limited
London, Colchester and Beccles

This paperback edition is distributed in the USA by
Harper & Row Publishers, Inc., Barnes & Noble Import
Division. A hardback library edition is distributed in the
USA and Canada by J. B. Lippincott Company, Philadelphia
and Toronto.

Contents

v

Contents

Contents

Part III Implications and Conclusions

Figures

ix

Acknowledgements

The pilot study that produced this book was carried out between 1966 and 1969 under the sponsorship of the then Ministry of Health (now merged into the Department of Health and Social Security). We are indebted to the Ministry not only for financial support but for the advice, interest, and encouragement of its officers throughout the project. Thus although we were explicitly given freedom at the outset to publish our findings, we were glad of the opportunity to submit a draft of this book to them and to receive their comments and suggestions. Responsibility for the result is of course entirely ours.

Similar interest and helpfulness were displayed in almost all the institutions we approached in the course of this study; and some had to tolerate repeated visits from us over a protracted period. We are extremely grateful to them and it is a pity that the need for anonymity prevents us from listing the institutions and individuals concerned. We have, however, mentioned in the text, and must single out for special acknowledgement, the Le Court Cheshire Home. It was a group of residents at Le Court who first persuaded us of the need for research into residential care for the severely disabled; and in the course of the project we collaborated with the Management Committee, staff, and residents in designing and implementing certain changes in the running of the home. This experience was invaluable in forcing us to clarify our ideas and allowing us to begin to test them in a real-life setting; we welcome this chance publicly to thank all those involved for working with us. Whether because of or in spite of our interventions, the outcomes are generally agreed to be satisfactory.

Although we have the formal permission of Le Court to

publish the material derived from this experience, we would emphasize that (as with the Department of Health and Social Security) this does not imply endorsement of our findings. In fact, some of the residents who were kind enough to read and comment extensively on the draft disagreed with a number of our observations and inferences. In the final version we have taken into account some of their criticisms, but by no means all. Since it is our aim to stimulate informed debate on and the search for better solutions to the problems of residential care, we would indeed hope that the modifications we have made will not deter these critics from pressing their counter-arguments in public.

We also owe thanks to a group of heads of institutions who worked with us in the winter of 1966-67. They came to take part in what was intended to be an experimental form of training (referred to in Chapter 12); but as so often happens in such cases we may well have learnt more from the experience than they did.

Mrs Stella Thomas made a brief but useful contribution to the project by working as an aide in one institution and keeping a full record of her experience. To her, too, we are grateful.

Finally, we acknowledge the advice of a number of colleagues with whom we discussed the project. In particular, the late Dr A. K. Rice was an immense source of support, both in listening patiently to us in phases when we were depressed, confused, or both, and in helping us to understand and conceptualize the processes described in this book.

The Centre for Applied Social Research   E. J. M.
Tavistock Centre   G. V. G.
Belsize Lane
London NW3
April 1970

Introduction

CHAPTER I

The Design of the Book

OTHER STUDIES OF RESIDENTIAL INSTITUTIONS

Residential institutions have received considerable attention from social scientists in the past fifteen years. Much of this has developed from the concept of the therapeutic community. Following the pioneering work of Main, Maxwell Jones, and others (Main, 1946; Bridger, 1946; Jones *et al.*, 1952; Rapoport, 1960; Martin, 1962) it rapidly came to be accepted that treatment in a mental hospital does not take place only in the relationship between therapist and patient. The patient's other relationships in the institution may be just as significant, if not more so. The hospital, therefore, has to be conceived as a social system functioning in an environment, a system that is created and maintained by all its inhabitants, staff and patients alike. Psychiatrists, social anthropologists, and others have collaborated to try to understand the dynamics of such systems. The United States has produced a crop of careful studies which have illuminated the processes involved: for example, Stanton & Schwartz (1954), Belknap (1956), Greenblatt, Levinson & Williams (1957), Caudill (1958). Effectively harnessed, the processes can reinforce specific therapy and contribute to rehabilitation; uncontrolled, they may be anti-therapeutic and lead to the symptoms of 'institutional neurosis' identified by Russell Barton (1966). In *Asylums*, Goffman (1961) has described vividly and relentlessly the insidious phenomena of the 'total institution' which can defeat a well-intentioned strategy of treatment. In order to survive in a setting that removes the usual props of individual identity, patients learn patterns of subservience which reflect and reinforce the overwhelming power of staff.

Although mental hospitals have attracted the bulk of the literature on residential institutions, the same shift in philosophy, from a custodial to a therapeutic orientation, has spilled over into prisons and other institutions that deal with delinquents and there is an increasing number of studies in this field. Mounting problems of juvenile delinquency in Western societies have focused particular attention on correctional institutions for young offenders: see, for example, Street, Vinter & Perrow (1966).

The residential institutions with which we are concerned here – those for the physically handicapped and younger chronic sick – have not so far shared in this burgeoning of interest. There have been no practitioners to propound radically new approaches or social scientists to dissect them. Even Goffman, who in *Asylums* quotes from the literature not only about mental hospitals and prisons, but also about schools, ships, army units, and nunneries, has no reference to homes for incurables. Such books as exist have for the most part been written by the inmates themselves.

There are obvious reasons for this neglect. The number of inmates involved is relatively small – in this country a few thousands as against more than one hundred thousand in mental hospitals and penal or corrective establishments. Moreover, their disabilities, being physical, are perceived as being fundamentally more irreversible than those of the mad or delinquent. There is some reality in this, and it should be noted that the shift from custodial to therapeutic philosophies depends on the belief that these other disabilities are potentially reversible. Irreversibility and the institutional problems it poses are themes to which we shall return.

OUR OWN APPROACH

This absence of authoritative social science literature has not been wholly disadvantageous. It has given us no option but to focus on our own experience of the institutions we saw and worked with, and to distil what insight we could from it. We were not there to test hypotheses derived from the theories of others, but to try – within the limitations of a three-year study on a part-time basis – to tease out some theory of our own which would make sense of our observations and perhaps be of practical help to those who run institutions of this kind. To this end, although we had planned from the outset to pay brief visits to a large number of institutions and to study half a dozen in some detail, we were particularly anxious to work with at least one in an 'action-research' role. We believed that only by establishing a relationship within which we could feed back our preliminary findings to members of the institution, discuss and develop the concepts, and then collaborate with the institution in making changes, would we be able to come to grips with significant institutional processes. We did that, and to a major extent this book is the result.

A theory has two types of function. It selects from the welter of facts that crowd the specific situation certain significant variables and shows their relationships at a level of abstraction that allows the theory to be examined and applied in other situations. It puts distance, as it were, between the observer and the data. And it is this that leads to the second function, which is defensive: the individual who wields the theory can feel less involved, more detached, safer and superior on his higher plane. If the theory deals with the phenomena of inanimate objects, this defensive function is of no great consequence. If the phenomena are social and psychological, then it is of the utmost importance. Every individual is a theory-maker in the sense that he abstracts and stereotypes, and constructs hypotheses of cause and effect; and in so far as his theories of human behaviour are integral to his personality he is adept at testing his hypotheses in situations that are certain to confirm them. Social scientists are not immune from this process. Thus whereas it may not be of great relevance to inquire what motivated a physicist to explore the behaviour of electrons and neutrons, it is necessary to be a good deal more searching about the social scientist who studies, say, a mental hospital. What was his motivation? What prejudices did he bring with him? What was the nature of his role and of the relationships that he made? And, more fundamentally, what was he trying to defend himself from?

It may be contended that the theories of social science are

just as amenable to re-testing by others as are those of physical science, and that on this basis they can be accepted or rejected. This is true so far as it goes, but leaves out of account the fact that, since the social sciences are still relatively medieval, the theories that might be tested in this way are correspondingly trivial. As Janowitz (1966) and others have pointed out, the critical contribution of social science findings to institutional problems, as to other contemporary issues, is not through an 'engineering' model of social research – the mechanical application of an established body of theory – but through an 'enlightenment' model. In other words, we come back to the point that the principal criterion is whether the practitioner can make use of the new approach to enlarge his own theory of the situation he is in and to extend his competence. By whatever external criteria the theory may be judged 'true', the practitioner can use it only if it is 'true' for him. Theories that are apparently 'untrue' – in the sense of unconfirmed through scientific tests – may also be useful. For example, in an early study of a mental hospital Stanton & Schwartz (1949) identified a connection between disagreement among staff and turbulence among patients. Although subsequent research has not confirmed such a connection (cf. Dinitz *et al.*, 1958; Wallace & Rashkis, 1963) the notion that it may exist has probably broadened the theoretical perspective of many practitioners.

We have argued this point at some length in order to establish our own position. While we disavow the possibility of an objective approach to social research, we do not believe that non-objectivity invalidates the findings. But since we have had to go through processes of selecting and abstracting, and distancing ourselves to some extent from the data in order to arrive at any findings, evaluation of the results has to take these processes into account.

The second chapter of this Introduction is, therefore, devoted to a personal narrative of how we first became involved in this project, what our feelings were about it, and how our involvement and feelings changed as the work progressed. We include a description of the early stages of our action-research role in the particular institution, Le Court, since it was this that compelled us to try to distil something coherent and communicable from our observations and experiences. And, as we have said, the rest of this book is essentially the result of that distillation.

Such a personal statement is probably of greater importance in this study than in most, because of the stress we experienced in moving among the disabled inmates and trying to see the world through their eyes. We were subjected to many harrowing stories – of medical mismanagement, of broken promises and rejection, of social deprivation, of physical pain. The historical truth of these stories was unascertainable and sometimes suspect; the acute depression that underlay them was unmistakably true and communicated itself readily to the listener.

The problem of becoming personally involved with one's respondents was not, of course, new to us: it is inherent in our method of working (cf. Sofer, 1961). The way we have dealt with this in the past has been to accept that one uses oneself as a measuring instrument and to try to develop means of calibrating it so as to correct for some of the distortions. Personal psychoanalysis is one such mechanism. Discussions with colleagues not directly engaged in a project help us to identify our prejudices and to regain some detachment. When we dictate, into a tape-recorder, our records of meetings with respondents, we try not to inhibit spontaneity; we aim not only to convey the content of the discussions and the feelings that other people are expressing, but also to get our own feelings into the open. They can then be identified and taken into account when the notes are re-read later. The opportunity of working on other assignments – we are usually, as we were in this case, engaged on more than one at a time – also helps to maintain a steadier perspective.

These mechanisms for calibration are at best imperfect; but never have they been so severely taxed as they were during this study. We found ourselves subjected to pronounced oscillations of feeling. One day we would be overwhelmed with sympathy and pity for the plight of the disabled, doubly persecuted by their physical handicaps and by the destructiveness of the environment in which they lived. Next day we would see the staff as victims of the insistent, selfish demands of cripples who

7

ill deserved the money and care that were being so generously lavished upon them. Since we worked as a pair, our opposite oscillations sometimes damped one another. But if the oscillations coincided, we relied heavily on the intervention of an uninvolved colleague to restore some semblance of balance.

It is a slight consolation that we were not alone in this. Of the many people we met in the course of this study who were in one way or another concerned with the disabled population, we can recall none who was not either struggling with the ambivalence displayed in our own oscillations of feeling or else captured by a permanent bias.

Although, therefore, Chapter 2 is primarily an account of our own experience, it cannot be entirely dismissed as being concerned with the idiosyncratic responses of two observers. In part, certainly, our emotions were unique; in part they expressed values and attitudes that are widely prevalent among so-called 'able-bodied' members of society.

OUTLINE OF PART I

We take this point further in Part I, entitled 'The Context of Residential Care'. The theme of *Chapter 3* is that the cripple, whether in an institution or not, is an outsider. Almost every society draws a sharp distinction between its able-bodied members and its cripples. Generally the latter are despised, though in some communities they are given privileged positions and revered. Very seldom indeed are they accepted as people first and as cripples second. In our own society liberal values are gaining ground: it is becoming progressively less respectable to display intolerance or discrimination towards minority groups, cripples among them. In behaviour, however, discrimination persists. It is because of this discrepancy between professed values and actual behaviour that we prefer here to use the word 'cripple', which draws attention to the discrepancy, rather than such terms as 'a person with a disability', which make it too easy to ignore the social disabilities that accompany physical disability. Goffman (1963), for example, shows that discrimination in personal encounters between the 'normal' and the handicapped is almost inescapable. In the last section of Chapter 3 we consider some of the psychological consequences of the cripple's differential experience of others and also of his own body.

In *Chapter 4* we turn to the institutions that cater for cripples in this country. After discussing the various different types of residential accommodation that are provided, we go on to describe more specifically the five institutions on which our own study was focused.

Then in *Chapter 5* we bring together the cripple and the institution in their social context. We argue that the essential characteristic of the people taken into the institutions is not simply that they are crippled and, therefore, to a greater or lesser degree in need of physical care, but that they have been written off by society. To the extent that they are seen to be incapable of occupying any role that is positively valued by society, they are in effect socially dead. The definition of the primary task of the institutions that follows from this view poses immensely difficult, if not intractable, problems. Not surprisingly, therefore, institutions seek the defence of trying to operate on the basis of other, more innocuous, definitions. We outline the features of what we call a 'warehousing' ideology, based on humanitarian values, and a 'horticultural' ideology, based on liberal values, but suggest that both are used as defence mechanisms and that neither is quite appropriate to the real task that has to be performed.

OUTLINE OF PART II

To analyse the functioning of institutions and to make meaningful comparisons between one institution and another, we need a theoretical framework which will help us to understand and explain the ways in which different aspects of functioning are connected with one another. The framework we use in Part II is one that has been developed principally at the Tavistock Institute for the study of organization in a variety of settings, including industrial and commercial enterprises, research units, educational establishments, and therapeutic institutions, in which we have not only been involved in a research capacity but have been actively engaged in trying to help enterprises to discover more effective ways of performing their tasks. (See especially Miller & Rice, 1967. Also: Emery & Trist, 1960; Miller, 1959; Rice, 1958, 1963, 1965; Rice & Trist, 1952; Sofer, 1961; Trist & Bamforth, 1951; and Trist *et al.*, 1963.)

This framework uses the concept of an 'open system', which is borrowed from biology. All organisms and all enterprises have the characteristics of open systems. That is to say they exist, and only can exist, by exchanging materials with their environment. ('Materials' is used here in a very broad sense: it might include inanimate objects, organisms, or even ideas.) An open system imports materials; it transforms them in some respects by means of conversion processes; it may consume some of the products of conversion for the purposes of internal maintenance and it exports the rest. Directly or indirectly, it exchanges its output for further intakes, including further resources to maintain itself. These import, conversion, and export-cum-exchange processes are the work the enterprise has to do if it is to live. No enterprise is more than partially independent of its environment.

Every enterprise has a great variety of inputs and outputs – raw materials, finance, staff, supplies, information – and engages in a corresponding variety of conversion processes. At any one time the enterprise has a primary task, the task that it must perform in order to survive. This gives immediate priority to one specific process. Thus a hospital that is short of nurses must give priority to recruitment if it is to continue to exist. But if it is to remain a hospital and not to change into a different type of institution, the process that must remain dominant for most of the time is the treatment of patients. In the case of a manufacturing company, the dominant input consists of raw materials, which it converts into products (and waste). The returns it gets from selling the products enable it to acquire further raw materials, to maintain and develop the company, and to pay out dividend and interest to those who finance it. An airline takes in potential travellers and converts them into passengers who have arrived at the desired destination. A college takes in students and exports a proportion of them as graduates. Unless an adequate proportion of airline passengers consistently reach their destinations, and an adequate proportion of students graduate to appropriate standards, the enterprises concerned are likely to lose their future intake. Fares or fees will not be forthcoming; nor will finance from other sources.

Hospitals, airlines, and colleges, like residential institutions, are systems with a human throughput. Whereas the consumers that a manufacturing company has to satisfy are outside in the environment, these enterprises ingest, so to speak, a significant part of their environment into the core of the system.

One way of considering an enterprise or institution is, therefore, in terms of its throughput. Another is in terms of its resources – of finance, land, buildings, equipment, and staff. But what makes the enterprise a living system is the interplay between the resources and the throughput – the *activities* through which an intake is acquired, processed, and transformed into an output.

It is useful, sometimes essential, to think about activities independently of the means – the people or the apparatus – through which they are carried out. Only in this way can one devise new ways of performing these activities. For example, before a kidney machine could be invented, it was necessary to separate the idea of the kidney as an organ from the functions it performs, such as filtering impurities from the blood. Similarly, if one can think about teaching not in terms of 'what a teacher does' but in terms of specific activities required to 'process' a student (and the 'processing' can vary all the way from intensive coaching to the creation of a benign setting in which the student can find his own ways of learning and maturing), then it becomes possible to consider alternative means of carrying out the processes required.

In some manufacturing companies, automation now makes it possible to replace many of the human resources by machines. In residential institutions, mechanical devices are available to contribute to the processes of physical care or to make inmates more self-sufficient, and there is undoubtedly scope for greater use of such devices. Even so, the bulk of the 'processing' requires human resources to interact with a human throughput.

Human resources are much less tractable than machines. The factory may seek 'hands', but it recruits minds too. Like machines, employees often produce less than is expected of them; they also produce more. It is their versatile capacities and their needs, as individuals and in groups, that allow the enterprise to develop and indeed to exist; but they also bring with them capacities that the enterprise cannot use and needs that it cannot satisfy.

Dynamically, the individual may be regarded as having the characteristics of an open system. He has an inner world of thoughts and feelings that are derived from his biological inheritance and from what he has learnt and mis-learnt from his lifetime of experience; he lives in an environment to which he has to relate himself in order to survive; and it is the function of the ego – the conscious, thinking mind – to regulate transactions across the boundary between inside and outside. In the mature and healthy individual the ego distinguishes the realities of the external world from fantasies projected from inside; and the ego mobilizes internal resources of rationality and insight to deal with those realities.

Similarly, the sophisticated group develops means of internal and external communication through which it can perceive the external realities and the resources of its members and can mobilize their capacities in a collaborative effort. Each individual takes on a role, whether fleetingly or more permanently, through which he contributes activities that fit the overt purposes of the group.

But the individual also interacts with the group in ways that go beyond these overt purposes, sometimes reinforcing them, often obstructing them (cf. Bion, 1961). He carries inside him and brings with him to each new group the experience, satisfying and frustrating, of all the other groups of which he is or has been a member, starting with the family in which he was born. In relation to a new boss, or to new colleagues, his expectations and behaviour are conditioned by all his previous experience of corresponding relationships, including his earliest experience of his parents, or of brothers and sisters. Memories of the past modify what he perceives, feels, and does in the present. The memories are unreliable, full of inconsistencies, and not entirely accessible to consciousness. Thus the member uses the group, and the group uses him, in ways of which he is unaware, to express views, play roles, take action. The individual may deal with inconsistencies within himself by projecting them into the group; while the group imposes its own consistency on him.

The resulting pattern is one of cooperation and conflict, first between the members as individuals and the group culture they have produced, and second between the sophisticated group, through which they collaborate to achieve an overt purpose, and that other group, ostensibly with the same membership, through which they simultaneously express their fantasies and assumptions about themselves and about each other.

Every enterprise, then, has to take account of these characteristics of the individuals and groups that comprise its human resources. In a factory, however, an unambiguous boundary divides the human resources from the material throughput that is being processed. In a residential institution, as in a college or an airline, both the resources and the throughput are subject to the same 'laws' of human behaviour. The boundary between them may easily become blurred, or else artificially accentuated; in either event, the many groups that comprise the resources and the throughput will interact with each other in complex and often unanticipated ways.

It is this interaction, in the context of the task of the institution, that we examine in Part II, as we consider the import, conversion, and export processes of residential institutions for the physically handicapped and young chronic sick.

Chapter 6 is concerned with the import process. We discuss the different ways in which the institutions control admissions. Attempts to control this boundary pose certain dilemmas. The criteria used are often as much concerned with protecting the selectors from their problem of rejecting many who are in need as with relating their available resources to the actual needs of those they admit.

The next three chapters are concerned with the 'conversion processes' of these residential institutions. All, of course, have to provide physical care. The problems involved are discussed in *Chapter 7*. We suggest that this process is appropriately defined in terms of providing for both physical and psychological dependency. Institutions vary greatly, however, in the extent to which they go beyond this and make provision for their inmates to occupy other roles besides that of patient – the extent, in other words, to which they provide for inmates to exercise independence. We suggest in *Chapter 8* that in the more effective institutions inmates not only are the throughput of a caring system but also have the opportunity to constitute part of the resources of one or more differentiated systems of activities, through which they can relate back to the wider society.

Although this can mitigate some of the disadvantages of institutionalization, there remains the underlying problem of irreversibility. For inmates who are, in our terminology, 'socially dead' at admission and whose stay in the institution will be ended only by physical death, the transition from the one state to the other can too easily become an ever-narrowing tunnel, unless special forms of support are available. These, however, as we show in *Chapter 9*, are largely lacking; and indeed in some cases the plight of the inmates seems to be the means through which support is secured for inadequate staff.

Chapter 10, entitled 'Export Processes', makes the point that realistically the export process is concerned with death. But the uncontrollability of such an export boundary leads to a defensive search for other tasks and other kinds of export – which in turn detracts from performance of what we would define as the appropriate task.

The implications of this task for institutional leadership are the subject of *Chapter 11*. Leadership straddles the boundary between an institution with one set of values and the wider society with rather different values. If the distinctive needs of inmates are to be met, these differences must be acknowledged. This suggests that the able-bodied person who occupies a leadership position should not derive his status solely or even primarily from this – he should also have firm roots in the community outside. It further suggests that inmates themselves can appropriately move into some aspects of the leadership role.

IMPLICATIONS AND CONCLUSIONS

In this last part of the book we draw together the threads of our argument and consider what options are open. We offer no panaceas, no easy solutions. As we have suggested already, the problems of providing residential care for the physically handicapped and chronic sick are in many ways intractable and will remain so until and unless there is a pronounced change in the values of society, which may make the parasitism of some of its members more acceptable to all.

Short of such a social transformation, or of medical miracles, there is nevertheless scope in many institutions for some development. As our work at Le Court and elsewhere has indicated, it is possible both to arrive at more effective concepts of residential care and to recruit staff and train them to operate more successfully.

CHAPTER 2

Encounter with Disability

THE FIRST CONTACT

Our involvement began in January 1962 with a letter typed on the paper of *The Cheshire Smile: The Quarterly Magazine of the Cheshire Homes*, and gave the address as: Le Court, Liss, Hants. Printed on the right-hand side of the letter-heading was a drawing of a megalocephalic smiling cat, sitting in a wheelchair:

'Dear Dr Miller,

Mrs R . . . suggested I should send you a copy of this article I have written for the spring issue of the Cheshire Smile.

If you are interested in it, we wondered whether you would be able to come down and discuss the subject. The Editor . . . has for some years been keen on the idea of using the Homes as therapeutic group communities, since they seem ideally suited to it in many ways. . . .'

The article was entitled 'Oiling the wheels' and plainly had been written by someone informed in the fields of social and individual psychology. It pointed out that Cheshire Homes provided 'a nearly-normal life for people too disabled to manage independently' and that community life could be most rewarding. But the 'strains and hazards of group association' also posed difficulty. It went on to make a convincing case for securing the services of trained social workers 'to help people in adjusting to their disabilities and to each other'. In conclusion: 'When such great strides are being made in group dynamics and social psychology it seems a pity to neglect the opportunity of oiling the wheels of the machinery of this new venture in community living.'

A second letter filled in more details. Some three years previously, it said, a group of residents at Le Court had tried to get a social worker in a research role. An approach had been made at that stage to the Tavistock Institute, but nothing had come of it. The late Sir Ernest Gowers, then chairman of Le Court's Management Committee, had tried to get something done through the London School of Economics; but 'there was no one with enough interest and enthusiasm to carry it through'. The letter went on to say that the reading of a book by Elliott Jaques, *The changing culture of a factory*, had suggested that the Tavistock Institute could 'be of immense help'. The invitation to visit Le Court was reiterated and the concluding sentences of the letter further baited the hook:

'It is a particularly crucial time just now as our Matron is leaving to get married and the Secretary is also leaving. Both have been with us for more than four years, so there will be a period of readjustment in which we could do with help and which might also be an opportunity for change. Also the Residents' Welfare Committee will be changing at the end of the month, and for various reasons there is likely to be a period of transition in its affairs.'

The reply to this letter was not overly enthusiastic:

'... My colleagues and I ... are working under considerable pressure ... and I do not foresee the likelihood of our having a research worker available. ... May I suggest that if you are going to be in London, you come in for a discussion. ...'

The response was forthright:

'... We should very much like to come and see you. ... As we are all in wheelchairs perhaps it would be as well if only Mr S and I came. It would be quite an undertaking, since Mr S's chair is a long one, and I think we should have to arrange for two cars. ...'

And this evoked a much more conciliatory answer:

'... I recognize how inconsiderate I must have seemed in suggesting that you came to see me in London. I am afraid I didn't realize it would be such a difficult undertaking. ... Could I suggest as an alternative that I visit you at Liss. ..?'

– and the visit duly took place in the spring of 1962.

This brief correspondence illustrates in miniature many of the difficulties that bedevil transactions between the disabled and the world outside. Of course the problems of such residential communities are socially important and technically interesting; but a great many other problems always seem to have priority. That the disabled should themselves be talking about their needs in terms of group dynamics and therapeutic communities (and using these terms not just as catch-phrases but as concepts) was not really to be believed. Conventional prejudices – so insidious that we are scarcely aware of them – had made it obvious to assume that the letter-writer was something to do with the management of the home, or perhaps a well-read, public-spirited citizen living in the neighbourhood. Consequently, the discovery that this was actually an inmate caused shock and guilt; and the last letter offered reparation by return of post. But such reparation does not betoken unalloyed love and empathy for the disabled: there may well remain – and the evidence of introspection suggests that there persisted for a long time in this case – an underlying sense of having been caught, together with a corresponding wariness about being drawn further in.

That first visit to the Le Court Cheshire Home was disturbing. 'A long, low, fairly modern building, it lay in a large estate with a commanding view over an unpopulated Sussex landscape. A beautiful setting – but, as one was quickly told, 'You can't converse with the cows'. Meeting the residents sharpened one's ambivalence. There were about forty, almost all severely crippled. It seemed impossible that one would ever be able to cross the barrier of deformity and disfigurement to communicate with the people beyond it; and one could feel that society was not unmotivated in isolating this community as far away as possible from 'normal' neighbours. Yet there was a strong opposing pull, a compound of guilt, compassion, and empathy, and this was reinforced by the recognition that if one could shift one's focus and see across the barrier one was meeting some highly intelligent and insightful individuals.

Certainly, what the residents spoke about on that first visit was not the capacities they lacked, but the difficulties of making

18

the fullest use of those capacities that remained to them. They were conscious that the dependence which in some areas of their lives was complete and inevitable spilled over into other areas where it was not. Institutional life reinforced their dependence in a way that deprived them of the rights and obligations of other adults to make quite ordinary decisions about their own lives – even such apparently trivial decisions as when to go to the bathroom. Correspondingly, the imminent change of staff was especially disturbing. It could so easily lead to the introduction of new routines, which would disrupt the fabric of habitual expectations of everyday life, and of different values, which might more subtly strip the residents of the hard-won elements of personal autonomy to which they clung.

Problems of this kind – and these are only examples – could not but capture our attention. The Tavistock Institute describes itself as being concerned with advancing the social sciences in the service of practical affairs of man. Here was an area that promised both a theoretical and a practical pay-off. Although there was some reality in saying that we were 'working under considerable pressure', time was nevertheless somehow found to discuss and think about the issues involved. One theme that interested us, for example, was that in contrast to most institutions with a human 'throughput' – airlines, hospitals, colleges – where inmates are transient and staff relatively permanent, in institutions for the disabled and chronic sick the position is reversed; yet it was the staff – the transients – who still had the determining influence on the culture of the establishment. A colleague, Robin Higgins, published a paper about this in *New Society* (Higgins, 1963). We read what we could of the relevant literature; we began to meet other people who in one way or another were involved in the field; and we kept in touch with our original correspondent.

From this source we were subjected to an unrelenting pressure, overt and covert, to get us to undertake practical research. That we were ambivalent about this demand is shown by the contrast between our expressions of concern and our slowness to act. Finance for research is hard to come by and it takes considerable time and effort to formulate a convincing research proposal; but there is little doubt that our delay in trying to find the money reflected underlying hesitations about what we would be letting ourselves in for.

Not until August 1965, three and a half years after the first contact, did we make an approach to a foundation. Although this failed, the Ministry of Health became interested and at the end of March 1966 confirmed that it would meet the cost of the pilot study we had proposed.

THE AIM OF THE PILOT STUDY

Our area of interest has already begun to be made explicit in the preceding pages. An initiative had arisen in one home; but the problems posed were plainly relevant to the many other institutions that provide long-term – usually life-long – residential care for those who, because of chronic illness, physical handicap, or both, cannot look after themselves or be looked after in their own homes. Progress in providing residential care has been uneven and there are still many who need it for whom it is not available. One often hears, for instance, of young chronic sick patients with active minds languishing among senile neighbours in the geriatric wards of general hospitals. But it appeared to us that we were moving into a new phase, in which the basic problems of providing shelter and physical care were at least in sight of solution. For some inmates these benefits were enough in themselves and something for which to be unequivocally grateful. After painful experiences of isolation and insecurity they could now be dependent, without further anxiety or ambition, in a dependable environment. For others, however, once their basic physical needs were satisfied, new problems of a psychosocial nature were beginning to arise.

It has long been recognized by sociologists that institutional life in itself tends to stunt and distort the personal development of inmates. Institutionalization, with its symptoms of apathy and withdrawal, is now almost recognized as an illness in its own right. But it is easier to diagnose than to prevent or cure. The group of residents at Le Court were concerned about this phenomenon not merely for themselves but for many less fortunate inmates elsewhere, who were less articulate about their condition. What could be done about it? Every type of residential institution, of course, has its crop of horror stories about sadistic staff (for a recent exposé of geriatric institutions, see Robb, 1967). The presenting problem for us, however, was not deliberate sadism, which, though appalling, seems rare,[1] but the well-intentioned managements and staff whose behaviour nevertheless appeared to compound the negative effects of institutionalization rather than alleviate them. Very infrequently one heard of the reverse; how and why this happened was obscure.

What we proposed, therefore, and the Ministry of Health accepted, was a pilot study which would have two components. These were, in general terms, to identify more precisely what was involved in providing residential care for incurables, and to discover possible ways through which appropriate changes could be brought about.

So far as the former component was concerned, the kind of data we wanted could not be secured by a survey of a large sample of institutions. Normal survey techniques are well suited to collecting uncontroversial factual information and, if carefully used, data on opinions and attitudes. What we particularly wanted to examine was the interplay between attitudes and behaviour. The opinion I profess in answering a questionnaire may be quite inconsistent with the attitude implicit in what I actually do. We therefore elected to sacrifice the representativeness of a larger sample in the interest of concentrating in greater depth on half a dozen institutions. We wanted to find out what problems were being encountered in different kinds of setting and the different ways in which they were being tackled (or left untouched or even unnoticed).

The second component was essentially action research. We planned to find one or two institutions in which changes were

---

[1] It must be stated that many inmates would contest this. For example:
'You always get sadistic people going into institutional work, whether it be prisons or homes, . . . where they're in a position of power, and whether they have an opportunity to exercise their sadism depends largely on the climate in the institution. . . . The bigger the institution, the more likely it is that a great deal of sadism goes unrecorded. . . .'

being carried out or contemplated and to work with the people concerned in dealing with the processes of implementation. This approach has several merits. In the first place, changes, or attempts at change, often reveal facets of a social system that, though critical, are not normally visible. Second, the institutions selected could provide real-life laboratories in which, with the consent of those involved, hypotheses emerging from the research could be tested. Third, the experience gained from taking part in these specific change processes might be communicated in a way that could be used by others who wanted to initiate changes elsewhere.

FIELDWORK AND ATTENDANT PROBLEMS

In the first phase of the pilot study we visited more than twenty institutions. They ranged in size from small units or special wards for a dozen inmates to large complex establishments accommodating 200 or more. Our aim was to find out, in a rough and ready way, what were the main differences between them and along what dimensions, so that we should have a better basis on which to select the small sample that would agree to a more detailed study.

About this there was no difficulty. Indeed, the majority of those we visited wanted to be included on the short list. This willingness reflected the very real concern shown by most of the people we met about the formidable problems they were faced with in trying to run institutions of this kind.

Altogether five institutions were studied. Work with two began in the summer of 1966, with a third in the spring of 1967, and with the remaining two during 1968. In each case visits were spread out over a protracted period – in the earlier ones, much more protracted than we originally envisaged.

One reason for this was a progressive development and refinement of our ideas about the kind of data we needed to collect. We started by using open-ended interviewing techniques. Focusing usually on the life-history of the individual we tried to elicit the issues that were of primary importance to him. We gained additional data by observing the day-to-day activities (and inactivity) of inmates, by attendance at meetings, and by scrutiny of records. People in managerial and staff roles, as well as some voluntary workers, were interviewed in addition to inmates. Another source of material was a journal kept by a mature university student whom we paid to work as a helper in one institution (with the knowledge and consent of all concerned) for a month of her summer vacation in 1966. As a result of this early experience we were able to develop an open-ended questionnaire for use in subsequent interviews with inmates, and another for use with staff. Once these had been formulated they also provided a basis for re-interviewing some of the earlier respondents from whom certain information had not been obtained.

A second and no less important reason for avoiding concentrated periods of fieldwork in one institution was the strain involved. We are referring particularly to the strain on the interviewer. This is not to discount the strain on some of the respondents, who quickly became tired: thus interviews had to be spread over two or even three separate sessions. Speech defects sometimes made the discussion very protracted. Occasionally they were so gross that the words were incomprehensible to the unattuned outsider and a fellow-inmate had to be drafted as an interpreter. A few inmates had no speech at all and we had to rely on securing information about them from other sources. Conditions like this were difficult for the interviewer too; but even more difficult was the content of the interviews. We have already spoken of the moving stories we listened to, of the depression we absorbed, and of the problem of preventing our emotions from swamping our wits. Spacing the interviews and interspersing them with other work helped in this respect, although it could not solve the problem.

We believed that it was particularly important to acquire and maintain a balanced outlook if we were to be effective in the action-research phase of the project. In practice, it was only during this phase that we learnt how difficult it was to use our reason without denying the validity of our feelings and vice versa.

Introduction

It was in May 1966 that the Management Committee of Le Court agreed to our using that institution as the centre for the action-research phase of the project. By that time we knew, or thought we knew, a good deal about Le Court, which had been passing through a particularly turbulent phase in the preceding four years.

Le Court was the first of the Cheshire Homes, of which there are now some fifty in the British Isles and many more abroad. It owed its beginnings in 1948 to Group Captain Leonard Cheshire, V.C., who had become a national figure in the Second World War as a courageous bomber pilot and in 1945 was Britain's official observer when the second atomic bomb was dropped on Japan. (For biographies of Cheshire see Braddon, 1954, and Boyle, 1955.) He left the RAF determined to devote his life to more constructive causes. After failing in one experiment in community living he found himself almost by accident personally caring for a man who was in the terminal stages of cancer and for whom hospitals could do no more. Soon he discovered others in a similar plight. It became his objective (later embodied in Le Court's constitution):

'To provide . . . for the care, treatment and maintenance of the young chronic sick and permanently disabled of both sexes irrespective of creed.'

Le Court was to cater in particular for those who

'are willing to work insofar as their capacity permits and should be of such intelligence and ability as to benefit from the special facilities and atmosphere of Le Court. . . . Persons suffering from infectious diseases or TB and persons of unsound mind shall not be eligible.'

It was also to be a home rather than a hospital,

'. . . the patients being encouraged to take whatever part they can in the day-to-day running of the home.'

In the early years Cheshire was heavily dependent on the goodwill of local people. They made gifts of furniture and

24

bedding; they helped with the repairs to the dilapidated building; they washed and mended clothes and they also helped to nurse the patients. The practice of involving local volunteers in the work of Le Court and other Cheshire Homes has continued ever since. Those patients who were able to do so assisted with the household chores.

A principle established during this early phase was that a Cheshire Home is a home for life. Inmates were to have security of tenure so long as the home itself survived. By 1954 the survival of Le Court was assured. With the help of a large grant from the Carnegie United Kingdom Trust, a new purpose-built home was in use. There was a cadre of trained nursing staff. The Cheshire Foundation was by this time in existence and through it Cheshire was establishing new homes in other parts of the country. Responsibility for the management of Le Court was formally delegated by the trustees of the Foundation to a local Management Committee which had been set up in 1950.

Given this more stable basis the home began to develop in new ways. The term 'patients' implies passivity and it is no accident that during the next phase the inmates insisted on being called 'residents', for their activity both in Le Court and outside was substantial. Internally they began to take on some of the jobs that had previously been the responsibility of staff. By 1959, for example, they were running a workshop; those who were proficient in one craft trained newcomers. They were also operating a shop on the premises and arranging their own outings.

Externally they were taking on an increasing amount of public relations and fund-raising work. They formed a film unit to record and publicize their own experiences of disability and their use of technical aids to overcome it as far as possible. Films of this nature were used for fund-raising and teaching purposes and also gave (to quote the title of one film) 'Living proof' of what could be achieved by the disabled. An organization called Holidays for the Disabled, which currently arranges an annual holiday for several hundred handicapped people all over the country, was started by a Le Court resident in 1961.

25

This same resident started the first support group in 1958. An active Residents' Welfare Committee founded the Le Court Association in 1963.[1] This was a particularly interesting venture because it demonstrated that residents were taking the initiative in recruiting supporters in the county and also because in 1963 the Executive Committee of the Association was the one official body where representatives of management, residents, and outside people could meet together.

Residents at this time were well aware of the benefits of living at Le Court. Le Court provided (to quote from an article by one of them):

> 'surroundings where people previously regarding themselves as unwanted clinical material or social outcasts can learn to reach towards full living and often attain horizons of personal and social achievement that would have been impossible had they never become disabled.'

As was shown, however, by the approach to us in 1962, they were also becoming aware that living in a community presented problems with which they did not find it easy to come to terms. In particular, they were anxious about the precariousness of such autonomy as they had managed to win for themselves. They recognized that they were lucky to have so much more freedom and opportunity for achievement than the inmates of most other institutions and at the same time they were afraid that given a change of staff many of their privileges might be arbitrarily curtailed.

These fears proved to be well-founded. That year (1962) saw the departure of a matron who had been at Le Court for five years. During her stay she had come to accept the special needs of an institution of this kind which contrasted so markedly with the hospital régimes to which she had previously been accustomed. In her own words:

> 'I have seen the need – it has been pretty well forced on me at times – to drop more and more of the defence mechanisms,

---

[1] Support groups contribute to the amenities of the home by raising money for specific projects. Each group is represented on the Le Court Association which acts as a coordinating body between the groups and Le Court.

the armoury, the inhibitions acquired during seventeen years of conventional nursing.'

In the eyes of the new matron, wedded to conventional nursing, the régime of Le Court was not merely liberal; it was anarchic. This view appears to have been shared by the full-time warden and by some members of the Management Committee. As a first step towards the restoration of discipline she and the warden imposed certain restrictions, principally on bedtimes and television viewing. Residents protested vehemently. They were perhaps protesting not so much against the rules themselves as against the arbitrary way in which they had been imposed, and more generally because they saw their fragile status as adults being eroded and their helplessness and dependence once again being underlined. Thus the question of the rules became a highly charged ideological issue. One was either for individual freedom or against it, for the residents or against them: there was no middle ground. Even though we ourselves were only remotely connected with Le Court at that stage we nevertheless found ourselves emotionally on the side of the residents. Physically they were totally dependent on the very staff members who were taking away their freedom. It was a situation in which mutual paranoia could be expected to escalate.

Within the home, residents' protests were disregarded and the warden then discontinued the practice of joint consultation with the Residents' Welfare Committee – a procedure that had been in existence for two years. Next, the issues were referred to the Management Committee. Residents proceeded to lobby committee members and friends in the neighbourhood who might be sympathetic to their cause. Management Committee, however, though internally split, backed the administration in threatening to remove first one then several residents at least temporarily to other Cheshire Homes. An appeal was then made to Group Captain Cheshire. He reassured residents that a Cheshire Home was a home for life and promised them security of tenure. At the same time he offered to find a house for those residents who wanted to take over total responsibility for managing a home of their own. At least a third of the residents

27

were interested in such a venture. Lack of funds ultimately
made it impossible, but even before this some residents were
questioning the advisability of the project, partly because they
regarded it as an alternative means of expelling the so-called
trouble-makers and partly too because total responsibility was
not what they were seeking. They hoped rather to create a
cooperative community with caring staff who shared the
residents' ideals.

'The troubles' continued for about a year. The new matron,
finding her position untenable, left, and efforts to find a replacement were unsuccessful. Eventually the immediate fears of the
residents were allayed by the appointment as matron of a sister
who had been nursing at Le Court for ten years. During this
time she had always been sympathetic to residents' demands for
self-determination. Several residents had urged her to apply for
the matron's post and were extremely anxious that she should
get appointed, and she also had some support among staff,
though the Management Committee was at first reluctant. At
all events it was clear that she would not arouse the kinds of
difficulty that her immediate predecessor had precipitated.
Indeed, throughout the three years during which she held the
post residents had no cause to complain that they were not
consulted.

Perhaps what was not recognized in 1963 was the effect that
the new matron's change in role was likely to have on her relationship with residents. In 1962 she had actively campaigned
on their behalf and identified herself with residents rather than
with staff. The position of matron required somewhat different
qualities. Sensitivity to and awareness of residents' needs was
a necessary qualification, but over-identification with them
could well be a handicap. Staff also had needs, especially in a
work situation of this kind which involved personal stress. The
nursing and domestic staff had to be led and their standards
maintained. Once she occupied an administrative post the new
matron must have found her position extremely difficult: her
personal satisfaction derived from work with residents; her role,
on the other hand, required that she took into account the
needs both of staff and of residents and reconciled any conflicts

between these that might arise. Her 'capture' by the residents did not leave her free to fill the role of matron and eventually she came under attack for failure in leading her staff. A potentially difficult relationship existed too between the matron and the warden, who had been on opposite sides of the fence during 'the troubles'. Both warden and matron had the difficult task of trying to operate on the boundary of the institution but over the years the warden had tended to move 'outside' while the matron was over-involved 'inside'.

Thus, although the symptoms of the crisis were alleviated by this appointment, it might be seen as buying peace from the residents at the cost of undermining the role of matron. For a more lasting resolution it was necessary to find mechanisms that would allow the residents to feel secure without making the 'boundary' positions of warden and matron so difficult to sustain.

The appointment of a new chairman of Management Committee in February 1965 marked the beginning of a period when such mechanisms were actively being sought and tried out. The new chairman, a barrister, came to Le Court with no prior knowledge either of the home itself or of the Cheshire Foundation (of which he was simultaneously appointed a trustee). Soon after his appointment he inaugurated meetings between representatives of Management Committee, staff, and residents to consider staff and resident representation on the Management Committee. The case for their representation on, or at least attendance at, Management Committee seemed to him, as a newcomer, overwhelming. A few members of the Committee said that they had held this view for some time but had been unable to get it accepted. As a trustee, the new chairman was in a more influential position. As a result of these joint discussions a recommendation was made to the trustees who agreed that residents and staff should each elect two representatives to sit on Management Committee for an experimental two-year period beginning in October 1965. It was hoped that this would break down the distrust which had existed for some time between residents and the Committee and between residents and staff and would also increase staff participation in the

29

affairs of Le Court. Fuller knowledge of decisions taken and the reasons for taking them was expected to avoid misunderstandings arising from rumours and from the passing of inaccurate or incomplete information. In fact, these representatives were not to become full members of Management Committee. Proceedings of the Committee were divided into two parts: Part II was devoted to issues affecting individual staff members and residents, when their personal backgrounds, financial position, and questions of discipline were subject to discussion; representatives received papers for and attended Part I only.

Apart from these important internal developments this was a phase in which the trustees of the Cheshire Foundation became much more active in relation to Le Court and made certain far-reaching decisions. The first move had come in November 1964 when Group Captain Cheshire announced to the Management Committee and to representatives of the residents that the trustees hoped to site the headquarters of the Foundation's Service Corps and its training school at Le Court. This was a new organization set up to recruit and train the staff for all the Foundation's homes. He proposed that it should be administered by the local Management Committee. Plans were also advanced for locating a post-polio respiratory unit for ten people at Le Court. A ballot was held at which the great majority of residents expressed their approval of the scheme. It was subsequently found that there was no particular demand for this facility, and a heavy-nursing unit to cater for a maximum of fifteen people (who might include some post-polio respiratory cases) was substituted. This latter development became a cause of considerable concern to residents who felt that they had been presented with a *fait accompli* which would dramatically change their home and which they were powerless to resist.

By the end of 1965 a new constitution was in effect which formalized the greater involvement of the trustees. It stipulated that up to a quarter of the Management Committee should be nominated by the trustees, and the home was designated 'The Cheshire Foundation Home'. It was to become 'the centre where the trustees can experiment with new ideas' and as far as possible it was to be 'the model of what the Foundation is

30

trying to achieve'. Le Court was the first Cheshire Home and over the years had prided itself, quite justifiably, on being an experiment in social living in which residents' initiative had played a great part. Consequently, it was an obvious symbol of what the Foundation was trying to achieve. What gradually became clear, however, was that its adoption by the trustees meant a reduction in the autonomy of the Management Committee and of the home generally. Thus in some ways the very adoption by the trustees of Le Court as a model was liable to destroy or at least reduce those creative aspects which had made it outstanding.

INVOLVEMENT

Although we had talked about action research, in the initial arrangements we made with the Management Committee in May 1966 we assigned ourselves what seems in retrospect a remarkably passive role. We proposed over the next few months to interview substantial numbers of residents, staff, and Management Committee members, after which we would feed back our preliminary findings in the form of a working note. Our tentative conclusions would then provide an agenda for further rounds of discussions. We accepted an invitation to be present as observers at meetings of Management Committee and its subcommittees. An issue that we did not raise was whether it was appropriate for our client to be the legally constituted Management Committee, consisting entirely of external members, or the amplified Management Committee, which included the staff and resident representatives. We tacitly accepted that it was the latter: we saw ourselves as collaborating with the institution as a whole in tackling its problems. What we were unable to acknowledge even to ourselves at this stage was that implicitly our 'client' was the resident group. It had been an initiative from one of the residents that had brought us into Le Court in the first instance and there was no doubt that residents looked upon us as their agents in helping them to secure a better deal and that we ourselves had tacitly accepted this definition of our role.

It rapidly became apparent that we knew a good deal less about Le Court than we had believed. Our work there was punctuated by crises which rudely jolted us out of some of our preconceptions. The first crisis occurred at the second Management Committee meeting that we attended. In Part II of the meeting, after the resident and staff representatives had left, the decision was made that the matron should be asked to tender her resignation. To us this was quite unexpected. She had been under personal stress, which must have affected her work, and six months previously had offered to resign, but at that time had been asked to stay. This was the matron who had been appointed after 'the troubles'. Her record during her thirteen years on the nursing staff had been one of devotion to the residents and sympathy with their wishes to participate in the running of the home. Her identification with the residents and her 'capture' by them had made it difficult for her to command the support of staff and of Management Committee. It now appeared that so far as the residents were concerned she had served her purpose and they too had withdrawn their support from her.

In the interval before the appointment of a new matron residents began to express increasing anxiety and insecurity about the decision. The principle of participation in management had been important to them, not only because they felt they had a contribution to make in this area but also because they hoped that by this means they would be in a position to curb the power of staff, and prevent it from being abused. Power, not unnaturally, was a major preoccupation with residents: because of their physical and economic dependence they saw themselves as being at the mercy of others. Events in 1962-63 had made them increasingly conscious of the need to ensure that the liberal tradition built up at Le Court should be safeguarded against the appointment of senior staff who might subsequently prove unsympathetic to residents' taking an active part in the affairs of the home. Newcomers to the nursing staff were thus invariably regarded with suspicion until they had proved that they were able to dispense with the authoritarian hospital tradition.

While we understood the anxiety that residents professed, we could not reconcile it with their action, since they had been instrumental in bringing about the resignation of a matron who had allowed them the very opportunities for joint consultation that they had sought. It transpired that one or two residents had complained to the chairman of the Management Committee about the matron's incompetence and but for this he would not have taken the initiative in asking her to leave. The residents, therefore, had brought this anxiety and insecurity upon themselves. They gloomily repeated rumours that a particular member of staff whom they looked upon as being out of sympathy with their cause had designs to take over. It was as if the prospect of actually achieving the ends for which they had been campaigning over several years was too threatening: they needed to get back to a position that would justify their paranoia and feelings of helplessness. At this time even those staff who had previously shared the residents' views were as puzzled as we were by their reactions and concluded that they were perhaps more interested in continuing a fight than in achieving a constructive solution.

The new matron, appointed from outside, took office in October 1966. But while this was the most momentous staff change in this phase it was not the only one. The warden's wife, who had been acting as secretary, was redeployed as housekeeper and a new secretary was appointed. (Later the warden's wife withdrew from the housekeeping role on grounds of ill health, and responsibility was transferred to the matron.) Since the warden himself was a newcomer who had joined only in April 1966, Le Court had a complete change in senior staff in the space of six months. Shortly afterwards two further changes nearly occurred: both the warden and the new secretary offered, but subsequently withdrew, their resignations.

It was in this fluid situation that we were trying to make sense of what was going on around us and to find a way of working with the people concerned. If the residents were paranoid at this stage they were not the only ones. We felt as if Le Court was creating chaos in order to prove that it was impossible for us to understand the situation and to be of help. Clearly we could no longer cling to any simple preconception that the residents were an impotent and helpless group thwarted by the prejudices of the able-bodied; yet it was not easy to find a more realistic and coherent theory to take its place.

We finally completed our first working note in December 1966. It was distributed to all members of the Management Committee, including staff and resident representatives, and to the warden and matron. In that first note we were still fumbling towards the conception of residential care that is expounded in this book. The principal point we made was that the problems within the institution arose from an unresolved conflict between two different notions of its task which were perceived as incompatible. One view was that the primary task was *to provide care*. As the first constitution showed, this was incontrovertibly the purpose for which Le Court had come into being. Controversy arose, however, over the interpretation of 'care'. Residents argued that staff frequently interpreted this task in repressive terms by denying them self-determination in those areas of life in which they were capable of exercising independence as individuals. Accordingly the residents emphasized that part of the constitution which stated that Le Court was intended to cater for those who could take part in its affairs, and to be a place where their 'remaining capacities' could be developed. They contended that care was incidental, therefore, to the 'real' task, which was *to cater for development*.

Corresponding to these two definitions of the task we could identify two separate organizations in Le Court, each acting on the assumption that the other was jeopardizing the real purpose of the institution. The formal organization was along traditional hierarchical lines. The trustees of the Cheshire Foundation delegated authority to the Management Committee, which in turn delegated responsibility for the day-to-day running of the home to the warden. The Management Committee experiment had not altered the formal structure of authority. Such an organization, while tailored to effective performance of the task of care, made little allowance for the development task. This latter task had over the years become firmly vested in an informal organization of residents whose voice was the Residents'

Welfare Committee. There was no staff leadership for this task.

One of the inferences we drew in the note was that the warden's role as head of the home and representative of the formal organization put him into an unenviable, if not impossible, position: he was held responsible for the two tasks of care and development of which the former, though nominally under his command, was actually under the professional leadership of a matron who had her own direct link with Management Committee, while the latter was virtually outside his control.

Working Note 1 was due to be discussed with the outside members of the Management Committee at their January meeting. Instead, another item took precedence: it was proposed that the warden should be asked to resign. There was a striking similarity between this incident and the earlier discussion about the matron six months previously – even to the extent that the warden too had offered his resignation a month or two before this meeting, though in this case he had withdrawn his resignation himself. It was plain to us that the deficiencies being attributed to the warden, as in the case of the matron, were not all personally attributable to him but belonged also to the nature of his role and of the institution as a whole. To this extent any hope that to get rid of the warden would get rid of the problems was illusory. In other words, we were again, it seemed, at the centre of another process of scapegoating.

Yet although we could see this, we were totally unable to communicate it. This is not to suggest that we might have intervened in order to defend the warden's position. It was probable that by this stage the process had gone too far to be reversible. Belief that a person is ineffective can, if it is reiterated often enough, become a self-fulfilling prophecy: he becomes, in fact, ineffective. What was disturbing nevertheless was our sense of immobilization, of impotence. We had collaborated effectively before in many different types of enterprises on problems of growth and change. For the time being, however, all our previous experience seemed to be nullified. It was as if the disability of the inmates had been transferred to us: we were crippled too.

As a result of its discussion, Management Committee agreed, though not unanimously, to seek the warden's resignation. After the meeting individual members conveyed to the chairman further misgivings about the wisdom of the decision; in particular, they doubted whether as a Committee they had adequately supported the warden in his role. Implementation was therefore postponed until after the February meeting when the decision was debated again and finally ratified.

It was at the end of this long meeting that our working note came up for discussion. Introducing it we suggested that there might be a connection between these crises over senior staff and our involvement in the affairs of Le Court. It was as if we represented a threat of change to which the institution responded with the message that the real problem lay with certain individual staff members: if these could be got rid of all would be well and no real changes need be made. Although this connection was dismissed as speculative and fanciful, Le Court's proclivity to engage in processes of scapegoating was not denied. We developed this theme, much as we have done in a later chapter in this book, relating the scapegoating to the extreme difficulty for an institution of this kind, in which so many inmates suffered from progressive diseases, to confront the central problem of deterioration and death. The notion that such an institution should and could be 'a happy home' was facile and unattainable. It led to feelings of impotence and failure among those who tried to work with the inmates and it also evaded the realities of the situation so that a great many of the issues that arose in the home were exaggerated and distorted.

Although there was little discussion of the working note as such, this interpretation of the scapegoating process seemed to be received by the Committee with considerable relief as if it went some way towards explaining their failure at times to translate good intentions into effective action, and perhaps it helped them subsequently to look more realistically at their task and role.

OUTCOMES

This is not the place for a detailed account of the remainder of our work with Le Court. After a round of discussions of Working Note 1, not only with Management Committee but also with staff and residents, we were able to clarify our ideas a little further. We then worked with the outside members of the Management Committee on a redefinition of the role of the warden and on the recruitment of a successor. We also collaborated in trying to clarify the relationship between the Management Committee of Le Court and the trustees of the Cheshire Foundation.

When we withdrew from a consultant role towards the end of 1967 we were still uncertain what, if anything, had been achieved as a result of our intervention. By the end of 1968, however, it appeared that a cultural change had begun to take place. To quote one resident:

'There's a stability and a sort of sense of security that we've never had before.'

Expectations throughout the institution had become somewhat more realistic. Residents as a group appeared to be more prepared to accept the shortcomings of individual staff members and less inclined to demand the impossible from them. Perhaps the quality of the new staff had improved as a result of better selection procedures; but, in addition, the existence of a clearer and generally accepted policy allowed the staff both to operate more effectively and to be perceived as doing so.

Among the residents there had been changes in leadership. Activities that had previously been the prerogative of a small elite were now being shared by people who were previously onlookers rather than participants. At the time of writing, residents are working with the Management Committee and staff on a new project to raise funds and extend the number of single rooms at Le Court. This appeal has given many people new roles and a new interest in the community.

It is most unlikely, however, that what has been achieved is a viable and lasting solution. In many respects the problems of

37

an institution catering for incurables are likely to be as intractable as the problems of the individual inmates. As our own experience taught us, there are no cures, no simple solutions. At first this seems a counsel of despair: there appears to be only a choice between preserving the fantasy and continuing to fail on the one hand, and giving up on the other. What our experience also taught us, however, is that this is not necessarily an 'either/or' situation. It is possible to accept the reality and to go on working at the difficulties that it poses.

PART I

The Context
of Residential Care

CHAPTER 3

Social and Psychological
Consequences of Disability

The notion that a person may have a physical disability but be normal in all other respects is appealing and has many advocates. Perhaps we are moving towards a form of society in which it will become more realizable. In the meantime it is a hope rather than a reality. The fact is that the cripple has to come to terms with much more than impaired bodily function. Society treats its crippled members differentially in a variety of ways and cripples have a differential experience of their environment and of themselves. Residential institutions for cripples, therefore, have to contend not only with physical disability, but also with the social and psychological factors that go with it.

Here we enter a jungle of stereotyped expectations and prejudices in which it is difficult to distinguish reason from rationalization, fact from fantasy. As we tried to show in the Introduction, we ourselves are none too certain of our own orientation in this jungle. As social beings we are, like cripples, caught up in the values of our society: we can try to identify our prejudices, state them and compensate for them, but this does not give us an objective orientation. We still, for example, have to write in the language of our society and that has its own landmines. The word 'cripple' is unacceptably pejorative to many people; and yet so many of the other possible terms use a negative prefix – *dis*abled, *in*firm, *in*valid, *de*formed – which serves to locate the cripple in society in terms of the absence of socially desirable attributes.

HISTORICAL AND CROSS-CULTURAL COMPARISON

Comparisons with other cultures can be of some help in understanding our own. In all societies the cripple is abnormal,

41

in the purely statistical sense of belonging to a minority group. His abnormality is usually visible. As is the case with other visible deviant groups, societies vary in the values, positive or – more usually – negative, that they attach to the physical abnormality in itself. Beyond this they vary also in the values they ascribe to roles that are either unavailable or exclusively available to the disabled.

The meaning that a society attributes to the cause of disability is closely related to the way in which the cripple is treated in that society (Wright, 1960; Hanks & Hanks, 1948). That is to say, if a physical disability is regarded as something that might happen to anyone, as a neutral phenomenon, then the cripple is less likely to be the object of discrimination. There are some primitive societies in which this is the case. Cripples are accepted and tolerated. There is emphasis on the obligations of the society to its handicapped members. The social pressures on the family are such that they cannot abandon the cripple and the option to terminate dependency lies with him not with the group. It would appear that in these societies, although the cripple may be denied a high status position, he is nevertheless accorded a role compatible with his capacities. In other words, the perception of the disability is realistic in that it does not 'spread' to include the whole person. According to Hanks & Hanks, such societies are characterized by an adequacy of economic resources, low competitiveness, and an absence of an authoritarian hierarchical structure.

More commonly, however, the cripple is marked out as deviant not only in physical but in other respects. The value assigned to physical deviancy is occasionally positive but much more often negative. In extreme instances this has led to the killing or abandoning of the crippled child, or at best to relegation to a most inferior status. At the other extreme, where abnormality has been equated with the possession of special supernatural powers, the cripple's status may be exceptionally high. Whether, however, the cripple is vilified or sanctified, the results are in one sense similar: he is perceived predominantly in terms of his disability and is stereotyped. Whatever his status he has been separated from ordinary people because he is physically different from them. Both perceptions, in other words, may be seen as a means of keeping the cripple at arm's length.

In the cultural antecedents of our own society there has been a persistent bias against physical deviancy. Examples are to be found in the Old Testament, in Greek mythology, and in Western European drama and literature since the Renaissance. The crippled villain has continued to appear in children's stories and contemporary comics. In earlier times physical abnormality was frequently associated with evil or sin. The association is clear, for instance, in the following quotation from Leviticus where the writer is establishing the criterion of physical perfection for the priesthood:

'None . . . who has a blemish may approach to offer the bread of his God . . . A man blind or lame, or one who has a mutilated face, or a limb too long, or a man who has an injured foot or an injured hand, or a hunchback, or a dwarf, or a man with a defect in his sight or an itching disease or scabs or crushed testicles . . . may not profane my sanctuaries' (Leviticus 21: 17-23).

The equation of physical defect with sin could lead to scapegoating of the individual in the belief that by this means the society would be restored to a healthier state. Frazer (1935, p. 255) mentions such a practice among the Greeks of the sixth century BC. When a city suffered from plague, famine, or other misfortune '. . . an ugly or deformed person was chosen to take upon himself all the evils which afflicted the community. . . .' After being publicly beaten, he was burnt and his ashes were cast into the sea.

In other cultures deformity is regarded as the consequence of misdeeds in a former life. This is so, for example, in Hinduism. Since it follows that cripples have brought their condition upon themselves, not only is sympathy considered out of place, but association with them is held to be dangerous: they are seen as a source of contamination. Despite their pariah status, they have a social function as beggars, for alms-giving is in itself believed to be virtuous and a means of helping the giver to escape from the cycle of reincarnation.

Sometimes the cripple has been allowed to take on a more privileged role that exploits his disability. The court jester is an example. His satirical comments on his masters were acceptable only because he could be laughed at as a person of no consequence. It should be noted that in our own culture until quite recently the cripple was a person to be laughed at and mocked; polite pretence that physical defects are invisible is a modern phenomenon.

THE CRIPPLE IN CONTEMPORARY SOCIETY

Barker (1948) has described the current position of the disabled in society as underprivileged, marginal, and involving new and unknown situations.

In many respects the cripple has 'never had it so good'. Public attitudes are less prejudiced, more enlightened. Children are taught not to laugh at cripples but instead to sympathize with them as unfortunate fellow-beings. It is part of the philosophy of the welfare state that society should provide for those of its members who cannot make provision for themselves and the postwar years in particular have seen an enormous growth in provision for the disabled. Special schools, often expensively equipped, cater for children who are too handicapped to enter ordinary schools. Sheltered workshops give employment in protected surroundings. Certain occupations (passenger electric-lift attendant and car-park attendant) are specifically reserved for those registered as disabled under the Disabled Persons (Employment) Act of 1944. For those incapable of working, social security benefits are available. Some local authorities – though not nearly enough – offer purpose-built flats or convert conventional accommodation for wheelchair users.

Yet the individual's experience is often one of discrimination and deprivation. In part, this is a product of special provision. Pupils in special schools may be brought up to believe that they will be able to take their place in adult society; but in fact only a small proportion get jobs and these are usually in the lowest income bracket. Sheltered workshops, though possibly the only means through which they can earn a livelihood, further cut them off from the world of the able-bodied. While the aim of social security is obviously to assist those in need, too often in practice the result is to push the cripple further out of the mainstream of society and leave him marooned on an island of poverty and dependency.

In this last respect the cripple shares the experience of other marginal groups – the unemployed, the aged, the homeless, the poor. (And often he belongs to one or more of these other categories as well.) Attempts to maintain some degree of independence are discouraged, even penalized: for example, a cripple who wishes to augment his income by working at home finds that as soon as his earnings exceed £2 1s. a week (in 1970) his social security benefit is correspondingly cut.

Beyond this, deep-seated prejudices, though verbally they may be denied, continue to find behavioural expression. Confronted with physical deformity most able-bodied people recoil and experience some feeling of revulsion however temporary or slight. Despite what they are taught, 'normal' children do not easily accept crippled children (Centers, 1963). Experiments confirm that the reaction of an able-bodied person to disabled people differs from his reaction to other able-bodied people: for example, his behaviour is more embarrassed, he terminates the meeting sooner and he expresses opinions which are less representative of his actual beliefs (Kleck, 1969). It is widely accepted that evaluative attitudes towards physique cause more suffering than the disability itself (Wright, 1960; Meyerson, 1948a; von Hentig, 1948). In fact, the social value attached to *mens sana in corpore sano* is strongly persistent and with it the corollary that an impaired body implies an impaired mind. We understand, for example, that most of the physical defects listed in Leviticus are still a bar to candidature for the Roman Catholic priesthood.

In small ways discrimination is a daily occurrence. It is commonplace, for example, for a cripple to be ignored and treated as a non-person ('How many lumps of sugar does he take in his tea?'), or to be regarded as incapable of comprehen-

45

sion. The obverse of this, a gushing sentimentality, may be equally difficult to bear, implying as it does the same devaluation of the cripple as a person.

Discrimination leading to outright and harsh rejection is reported most often from the world of work. Here an American with cerebral palsy describes his experience:

'With one extremely painful exception, as long as I was in the protective custody of family life or college schedules and lived without exercising my rights as an adult citizen, the forces of society were kindly and unruffling. It was after college, business school and innumerable stretches as a volunteer worker on community projects that I was often bogged down by the medieval prejudices and superstitions of the business world. Looking for a job was like standing before a firing squad. Employers were shocked that I had the gall to apply for a job' (Henrich & Kriegel, 1961, quoted by Goffman, 1963).

There is ample evidence of similar confrontations in this country (see, for example, Hunt, 1966, and Townsend, 1967). Disabled workers are almost unanimous in alleging that it is not enough that they should be as competent as their able-bodied colleagues: they have to demonstrate that they are more competent, more diligent, more conscientious.

The role ambiguities to which the cripple is exposed are thus considerable. He is told that he is worthy of substantial investment in special education and training to help him to adjust to a normal working role; and he is also told that he has no business to expect a job on normal terms. He can never be sure whether in a new social situation he will be accepted as a person with a disability or rejected and devalued as a mere cripple.

Goffman has described both the problems that are faced by cripples and other stigmatized persons in their encounters with 'normals' and the strategies that are used to reach a measure of adjustment. He goes on to say:

'The nature of a "good adjustment" is now apparent. It requires that the stigmatized individual cheerfully and un-selfconsciously accept himself as essentially the same as

46

normals, while at the same time he voluntarily withholds himself from those situations in which normals would find it difficult to give lip service to their similar acceptance of him.

Since the good-adjustment line is presented by those who take the standpoint of the wider society, one should ask what the following of it by the stigmatized means to normals. It means that the unfairness and pain of having to carry a stigma will never be presented to them; it means that normals will not have to admit to themselves how limited their tactfulness and tolerance is; and it means that normals can remain relatively uncontaminated by intimate contact with the stigmatized, relatively unthreatened in their identity beliefs. It is from just these meanings, in fact, that the specifications of a good adjustment derive' (Goffman, 1963, 1968 edn. pp. 146-7).

Earlier we commented that society assumes obligations to the disabled. We can now begin to identify what it is that society expects in return. Here are the views of two cripples:

'I also learned that the cripple must be careful not to act differently from what people expect him to do. Above all they expect the cripple to be crippled; to be disabled and helpless; to be inferior to themselves; and they will become suspicious and insecure if the cripple falls short of these expectations. It is rather strange, but the cripple has to play the part of the cripple just as many women have to be what the men expect them to be, just women; and the Negroes often have to act like clowns in front of the "superior" white race so that the white man shall not be frightened by his black brother' (Carling, 1962, quoted by Goffman, 1963).

'I think we felt in our hearts that the world didn't *really* expect us to earn our own livings; that if we did it would be mildly pleased and say how clever we were, but that if we didn't it would be neither surprised nor disappointed and would be quite willing to keep us alive in some fashion' (Battye, 1966, p. 13).

47

Battye clearly believes that society expects nothing in return; our own observations lead to a similar conclusion. If a cripple offers more than the nothing that is asked of him (apart, that is, from gratitude) he is contesting the values of society by expressing the extent to which he is similar to the able-bodied instead of being different.

In not expecting anything from the disabled, society infantilizes them and even forces them into a parasitic position. In this respect the socially sanctioned role of the cripple in our own society is not very different from that of the Indian beggar. The extent to which cripples are still implicitly devalued is more vividly illustrated by this non-role than by overt rejection.

Infantilization takes many forms. 'Treats' and outings laid on for the disabled are one example. This is not to decry the provision of such entertainment, but all too often local authorities and charitable bodies show greater readiness to spend money on arranging a fireworks display or some similar event for which ambulances and other specialized transport have to be provided than on equipment that might make an individual cripple a little more independent. Sooner or later most of the disabled find that it pays to collude with society. An example was recently reported in a national newspaper: three cripples from a well-known hospital wanted to attend a function in London but found that all the seats had been sold; they contacted the newspaper in question which asked the theatre manager if seats could not be made available. The manager complied, expressing himself as always ready to help in such cases. These cripples were asking for preferential treatment on the ground of their disability and the rest of society was only too prepared to entrench them in the dependent role. It is hardly surprising that the cripple who becomes conditioned to such indulgent treatment eventually demands it as a right while at the same time insisting that he wants to be treated 'as a normal person'. We noted an example of this inconsistent behaviour in a journal for the disabled in which a writer was describing an excursion to the seaside. She complained bitterly of discrimination in having been turned away from a restaurant where wheelchairs could not be accommodated and a little later was indignant at having been made to pay to go onto the pier instead of being admitted free.

We live in an age of increasing awareness of the needs and rights of minority groups. Undoubtedly attitudes towards the disabled are in process of change: the notion that a crippled child is a disgrace to be concealed from the neighbours has given way to public discussion of the problems and attempts at rehabilitation. Equally important, the disabled are attempting to gain recognition of themselves as a category with specific needs and are forming pressure groups to publicize these needs and to change attitudes. The foundation in 1966 of the Disablement Income Group to campaign for realistic pensions for the disabled is one example.

Yet it would be a mistake to read too much into these developments. In a society that is becoming more affluent and more geared to achievement it may well be that the advances the disabled are making do no more than maintain their relative position. It is still deeply discrediting to be non-affluent, a non-achiever, in contemporary society. Social discrimination, therefore, seems inescapable. As Barker (1948) says, the disabled generally, no matter what their individual achievements, are non-starters in a world geared to the needs of the able-bodied.

THE PSYCHOLOGICAL CONSEQUENCES OF DISABILITY

From what has gone before one would not expect the cripple to be psychologically untouched by his experiences. Research workers seem divided in their views on psychological effects: many point to some maladjustment on the part of the cripple, identifying certain characteristic unrealistic responses; others emphasize the occurrence of healthy development and good psychological adjustment. A summary of research findings (Barker, Wright & Gonick, 1946) identifies the age of onset, the severity of the disability, and the intelligence of the subject as crucial factors in adjustment. Those crippled early in life are said to show a greater degree of emotional immaturity and abnormal dependence on the family.

Adjustment, however, is a slippery concept. Assertion of individuality may all too readily be interpreted as maladjustment in a society in which the pressures on the cripple are to accept submissively a dependent role. It may therefore be more instructive to examine the kinds of experience of life that are particularly likely to have psychodynamic consequences for the cripple while at the same time recognizing that the extent to which he can come to terms with these and the way in which he does so will be affected by his own capacity for healthy development and by the support he receives from his immediate environment.

Here we consider, first, the effects of disablement in infancy and, second, the consequences of becoming crippled later in life.

Effects of Congenital Disability

The detrimental effects on personality development of early separation from the mother or permanent mother-substitute are well known (Bowlby, Robertson & Rosenbluth, 1952). Many of the children born with physical disabilities have to spend periods of their early life in hospital and are thus at risk in this respect. An increasing number of hospitals nowadays make provision for mothers either to accompany their children or to visit them frequently and to assist in their care. However, since orthopaedic hospitals serve large catchment areas, the practicability of frequent visiting is reduced.

Children consigned for long periods to hospital care may suffer emotional deprivation not only from the absence of parents but also from the impoverishment of the environment (Oswin, 1968) and the consequent lack of stimuli. Staff changes make it unlikely that a child will be able to build up a secure relationship with any of the nurses. The closer the tie he establishes with a particular nurse, the greater his pain at losing her. Withdrawal is one form of defence that may then be adopted. Another is an indiscriminate sociability which is both shallow and brittle.

Even if the child is not hospitalized, parental relationships may pose problems. The parents of a disabled child will already have internalized certain values about disability. If these are of

50

a particularly negative nature and if they themselves feel threatened by the appearance of deformity their reactions are more likely to be detrimental to the child than if they had achieved a tolerant attitude to abnormality. Outright rejection, however, is less common than over-solicitousness. Also, parental attitudes are frequently inconsistent and more extreme than they are towards normal children (Barker, Wright & Gonick, 1946). Some parents appear to expect the child's intellectual functioning to compensate for his physical disability, thereby creating additional stress in an already difficult situation. Some writers assert that personality and behaviour difficulties stem not so much from the disability as from the way in which children are treated by parents (Meng, 1938, Allen & Pearson, 1928, cited by Barker *et al.*, 1946).

The disability itself may nevertheless affect the child's body image and ego development. During his early life the infant is moving from a state of dependence and helplessness to one of relative independence and a degree of mastery over his bodily movements and surroundings. The infant whose motility is impaired will inevitably be at some disadvantage since sensorimotor activity is of crucial importance to the development of his ego (Kaplan, 1965; Burlingham, 1965). Through the movement of his limbs, through grasping and reaching for objects, and through perception of these movements the infant begins to distinguish the self from 'other' and begins to learn about his environment. It follows that reduced motility may affect the child's perception of himself, of the world around him and of his relationship to it.

Anyone with experience of small children will know the importance in their lives of movement and play activities. At this age play does not have quite the diversionary quality that it has later in life. Activities that adults regard as play are taken very seriously by the child: through them he learns new skills and enlarges his experience. At the same time, by gaining some control over his environment through play, his confidence progressively increases. Sensorimotor activities also enable him to canalize his aggression into coordinated activity (Loewenstein, 1950, cited by Kaplan, 1965) and he is therefore less overwhelmed by feelings of helplessness and anger. One of the effects of early crippling is a tendency for the child to acquire a superficial 'grown-upness' which is not based on real experience.

As a result of observing the movements and interrelations of different parts of his body, the child develops a body image (Kaplan, 1965), that is, an image of the body in the mind. The way in which a physically normal person perceives himself in imagination is likely to correspond to the reality of his physique. Difficulties arise when parts of the body are defective. The individual may then be unable to perceive his body realistically; instead he denies or enhances certain parts of it. The body may be perceived as made up of unrelated parts rather than as a whole. Incomplete or faulty knowledge of one's body tends to result in faulty general perception (Schilder, 1950; Kaplan, 1965). When the body image is distorted individuals may take refuge in beliefs of uniqueness and attribute quasi-magical properties to deformity.

Distortion of body image is thought by some researchers to be an inevitable outcome of early physical defect. Niederland (1965) undertook a prolonged intensive study of eight patients all of whom had small, not necessarily visible, deformities and were receiving treatment for psychological disorders. He found that they all tended to believe themselves to be exceptional and to have fantasies of grandeur. Although all showed impairment of object relations and reality-testing, they were also more creative than average. In addition they were characterized by excessive vulnerability and by aggressive demands on the outside world to feed their narcissistic needs. Although their psychopathology as adults appeared disproportionate to their minor afflictions, Niederland believed their disturbances were proportionate to their impairment in early life.

Even so, the psychological outcomes of early deformity are by no means thought to be irreversible (Meng, 1938, quoted in Barker, Wright & Gonick, 1946; Niederland, 1965). Lussier (1960), in the course of an analysis of a boy with severely shortened arms, found that his body image was realistic; the boy made constant (usually successful) attempts to compensate for his deformity.

Effects of Later Disablement

Whether an individual is suddenly crippled or discovers that he has a progressive disease which brings with it a gradual decline in capacities, he is faced with changes in his physical, psychological, and social conditions. As we have already indicated, the way in which he responds and the kind of adjustment he makes will depend on his own ego development, the internalized values he holds about physical impairment, and the response he meets from the environment.

When an adult is faced with a change in his body a period of shock, mourning, and depression will almost certainly occur. Indeed, absence of such symptoms may well hinder such processes of rehabilitation as may be realistic (Prosen, 1965). He may find himself unable to reach what were previously quite simple and easily achieved goals. Repeated experience of such failure may lead to lowering of morale, anger, resentment, or apathy. It may also lead to an experience of internalized failure (Meyerson, 1948a). He has to come to terms with dependency on others, though the extent of this may be diminished as he learns alternative methods of coping.

Obviously the experience of a person who is crippled as the result of an accident or poliomyelitis will differ from that of a person with a progressive disease. In the former case the change in condition will be sudden and dramatic, in the latter insidious. Although the progressive disease involves less dramatic changes, the individual has constantly to come to terms with both the actual and the prospective processes of deterioration.

RESPONSES OF THE CRIPPLE

The cripple has to contend, then, with three sets of problems. First there are those problems that arise out of the physical disability itself – the inability to achieve quite ordinary goals, the difficulty of establishing a realistic body image. The second set derives from the dominant mode of dependency – physical, emotional, financial – that the disability imposes on his relations with others. And, third, there are those problems that spring from the uncertain dependability of others who bring into their relationship with him social values and personal prejudices towards the disabled. These three types of problem are interconnected and reinforce one another. In so far as the able-bodied outsider, suffused by conventional attitudes towards cripples, responds to the disability instead of responding to the person, the cripple's own experiences of his encounters with the world around him are likely to be deviant compared with the experiences of the unstigmatized person.

Certain characteristic coping mechanisms may be identified. The cripple who unconsciously accepts a negative evaluation of himself is more likely to collude in a vicious circle of negative experiences until 'he slips into that minority complex in which people feel perfect and superior because they are maltreated and misused' (von Hentig, 1948). On the other hand, he may attempt to compensate by over-achievement: it is not enough to perform as well as the able-bodied; he must excel. Or paranoia, withdrawal, and denial may be adopted as defence mechanisms. As a result of past experiences of rejection the cripple becomes suspicious of the motives even of those who do accept him. He fears that the acceptance, instead of being genuine, is based merely on pity for his disability. The feeling that he is not accepted for himself leads to continual efforts to seek assurance from others or, alternatively, to aggressive behaviour in an effort to gain attention. Hostile and angry feelings as well as feelings of helplessness get projected into others; 'they' are said to be inefficient, unfeeling, or cruel. Another way in which an individual may respond to his disability is by denying it: while in the case of a slight disability this may result in good adjustment, in the case of more severe disabilities such 'obliteration' will lead to a greater or lesser break with reality.

To the extent that these responses are recognized as prevalent, the notion of the twisted mind in the twisted body gains credence. When, inevitably, it is carried into encounters between the able-bodied and the cripple, this hypothesis or dogma further distorts the relationship and makes it the more likely that the cripple will be perceived as, and will become in fact, deviant.

CHAPTER 4

A Sample of Residential Institutions

THE PROVISION OF RESIDENTIAL CARE

The total size of the crippled population in Britain is unknown. In part this is because physical handicap and chronic illness are hard to define; in part, too, because disability is still a discrediting trait which an individual or his family may prefer not to disclose to census-takers or other inquirers.

One might nevertheless think that it would be relatively easy to discover how many cripples live in institutions; but surprisingly this is not so. Early in our study we realized that even to try to establish the number of institutions catering for cripples would take up more time than we could afford. To obtain a preliminary picture of the field we therefore contacted a variety of relevant organizations and individuals and gradually compiled a list of our own.

Consequently, we cannot be sure that the twenty-two establishments we visited during the early months of the project were representative of residential accommodation in the country as a whole. Geographically, they were certainly not representative: to save time and cost, all but three of them were within fifty miles of London. Between them, however, they covered all the main types of institutional provision that are currently available.

Three of them were units operated by local authorities, catering for a total of ninety-three inmates. Two of these were modern establishments, purpose-built for a predominantly wheelchair population. The third was in a Victorian workhouse (now called an 'ex-Public Assistance Institution') which accommodated about 300 vagrant and unsettled men and included a cottage set aside for sixteen men with physical handicaps.

We visited five units run by Regional Hospital Boards, cater-

55

ing in all for 117 patients. Three were specialized wards for young chronic sick within large hospitals. They drew on hospital services and did not have the entirely separate complement of nursing and domestic staff that was found in the other two, which occupied converted houses. Two of the wards operated a six-weeks-in, six-weeks-out system, in order to maintain their patients in the outside community for as long as possible; but not all the patients came under this system and indeed one had spent thirty years in the same hospital.

The remaining two-thirds of the institutions were run by voluntary bodies, and it was here that we encountered the greatest variety. Some were sheltered workshops which insisted on certain minima of manual skills as a criterion for admission and sometimes for retention; some offered a home for life regardless of deterioration; some evicted inmates who became incontinent or mentally deranged; two were reserved for particular categories of disability (poliomyelitis and cerebral palsy); two fairly large voluntary hospitals favoured middle-class applicants and had substantial proportions of elderly inmates. Correspondingly there were big differences in the ratios of staff to inmates and in the proportions of professionally trained workers: one or two had only a single trained nurse on the premises.

The predominance of voluntary homes among those we visited probably reflects the proportion in the country at large. Voluntary associations have a long history of providing refuge for the aged, poor, and needy, including the disabled: for example, John Groom's Crippleage at Edgware and the Royal Hospital and Home for Incurables at Putney both date from the nineteenth century. Indeed, until fairly recently the homeless cripple who could not find a place in a voluntary establishment or gain admission to one of the rare free hospital beds had no alternative to the workhouse.

The last twenty years have seen substantial changes. By the National Health Act of 1947 the state took on the obligation to provide for those in need of medical and nursing attention. The National Assistance Act of 1948 made local authorities responsible for providing 'residential accommodation for persons who by reason of age, infirmity or other circumstances are in need of care and attention which would not otherwise be available to them'.

Changes in the age-structure of the population have led many local authorities to concentrate on provision for the elderly. But both local authorities and RHBs have also responded to increasing public concern by trying to cater for the distinctive needs of the 'younger chronic sick'. The terminology is clumsy. 'Younger' means under sixty – in other words, pre-geriatric. 'Chronic sick' is often attacked as misleading, since it tends to imply a requirement for medical and nursing resources rather than, as is often the case, for more straightforward help in getting dressed and going to the lavatory. Whatever term one uses, however, it is clear that the needs of this category differ on the one hand from those of the short-stay patients who comprise the majority of the hospital population and on the other from the often senile inhabitants of geriatric wards and old people's homes. From time to time the Ministry of Health has drawn attention to their special needs. For example, a recent circular (Ministry of Health, 1968a) pointed to the desirability of moving away from the dormitory or ward tradition to single rooms and mobile partitions as a means of giving these patients a degree of privacy in their communal existence. Even so (as an appendix to the same circular showed) one-half of these patients under the care of RHBs are in conventional geriatric or chronic sick wards.

But for voluntary provision, the situation would be far worse. Since 1948, when Group Captain Cheshire set out to create 'a home where residents might develop their remaining capacities and live as full a life as possible within the limits of their disability', there has been a remarkable increase in the number of homes for the younger disabled. Almost all of the fifty Cheshire Homes in this country fall into this category; and there are many others.

Taken as a whole, both statutory and voluntary bodies cater for a similar repertoire of physical disabilities, ranging from congenital conditions to progressive neuromuscular diseases, though the hospital system may have a somewhat greater concentration of people in the advanced stages of progressive diseases. With this possible exception, the type of institution to which a person is admitted often appears to be a matter of chance, depending on the network of referrals in which he finds himself.

Moreover, the correlation between type of institution and source of finance is not as obvious as it might seem. Local authorities may discharge their responsibilities under the 1948 Act, for example, by placing people in the care of voluntary homes. A voluntary home that meets certain standards in the numbers and qualifications of its staff can seek registration as a nursing home, in which case it may contract with an RHB to provide beds for chronic sick patients. (There were 299 such contractual beds in 1967.) Thus although voluntary homes depend on trusts, bequests, and donations for capital expenditure and for some additional amenities, many derive most of their running costs from the statutory bodies. To this extent they are providing a service to a client in the shape of a local authority or an RHB, and not simply to the crippled individual. We came across no inmate who was fully self-supporting: those who can afford it presumably find alternatives to institutional care. A number had some limited means of their own: in such cases the local authority demands and the voluntary home expects that the inmate will contribute towards his own upkeep. Both will certainly take most of his social security pension if he has one. The cost of patients in RHB establishments is borne wholly by the National Health Service. Here too, however, voluntary organizations play their part: there is usually a League of Friends or its equivalent to raise money for additional amenities, which may include ambulance or special buses for excursions, kitchen equipment, hoists, individual gadgets, and a variety of other items intended to make life easier for patients and staff.

Amenities apart, the actual maintenance cost per head in the institutions we saw ranged between £10 and £30 per week. RHB units were invariably the most expensive, and RHBs thus paid less for contractual beds than for their own.

58

SELECTION OF A SAMPLE

The heads of most of the institutions we visited were willing, even anxious, to be included among the five or six for more detailed study – which perhaps reflected their awareness of the special problems that arise in institutions of this kind. We therefore had considerable choice.

Apart from wanting to include in our sample each of the three types of provision – voluntary, RHB, and local authority – we were not concerned with representativeness. Indeed, since it was our aim to explore possibilities of raising the standards of care, especially in psychosocial terms, we were inclined to give precedence to institutions that seemed to be good of their kind, whether this was manifested in the dedication of the staff, the quality of the physical environment, or both. We were constrained, however, by distance from London.

We selected three in the first instance. The first voluntary home (VH 1 in the tabulations that follow) was inevitably Le Court, where the initiative had originally arisen. As a local authority establishment (LA 1) we chose a modern purpose-built unit in the suburbs. A young chronic sick unit in rural surroundings provided our RHB example (RHB 1). To these we later added a second voluntary home (VH 2), which had a reputation for progressiveness. And finally RHB 2 was included to exemplify the second main type of specialized RHB provision – a segregated ward for young chronic sick within a geriatric hospital.

Le Court was the oldest of the institutions, dating from 1948, and RHB 2 had begun catering for patients shortly afterwards. RHB 1 opened in the late 1950s. VH 2 and LA 1 both came into existence in the early 1960s.

In the next section we briefly describe the internal and external environments of each of these institutions and then give some comparative data on their inmates.

THE FIVE INSTITUTIONS STUDIED

Le Court (VH 1)

When the study began Le Court was in process of change with the addition of a separate unit for post-polio respiratory and other heavy-nursing cases. Accommodation consisted mainly of four-bedded rooms, with a few single and double rooms. Most residents used their rooms as bedsitters. Soft furnishings and colour schemes were matters of individual choice and all rooms, therefore, were different and tended to reflect the personalities of their occupants.

Public rooms comprised two TV lounges, dining room, library, and workshop, all with the exception of the workshop being on the ground floor. The entrance hall was large and provided a focal point – administrative offices, TV room, telephone kiosk, lift, and chapels led off it. Residents and staff frequently crossed this space on their way to ground-floor or upstairs rooms and it was unusual not to find groups of people using the hall as a kind of auxiliary sitting room. A terrace at the front of the building enabled residents to sit out of doors overlooking the grounds.

Le Court was somewhat isolated and its position at the end of a half-mile winding, hilly drive made it impossible for all but a very few residents to go out on their own. Links between the home and the neighbourhood were nevertheless maintained at both a personal and an institutional level. Residents ran their own bus and a car; the bus was regularly used for shopping in the nearest town and for any leisure outings that residents might arrange; the car was available for individual visits. Voluntary helpers enabled these outings to take place by acting as drivers or escorts. Voluntary workers also helped in a variety of other ways: in maintaining wheelchairs and devising gadgets; in decorating, sewing and mending, and flower-arranging; and in general care of residents (for example, assisting with baths).

Many of the staff lived in or were provided with houses on the estate.

The Second Voluntary Home (VH 2)

A large converted house in its own grounds in a prosperous residential suburb provided the setting for this home. Extensions had recently been added to provide as many single rooms as possible; most residents, therefore, had a room to themselves, which they were able to furnish as they wished.

The large hall and nearby sitting room were focal points. Residents invariably answered their own telephone and the front-door bell, and they looked after visitors. There was an air of activity and participation and, perhaps more than in any other institution we visited, one got the impression that this home belonged to the residents. The running of the work centre was their responsibility; part of the proceeds of the centre was used from time to time for improving the amenities of the home. Renewal of soft furnishings, alterations to the building, and other matters affecting the home were discussed in a House Committee comprising representatives of inmates, Management Committee, staff, and voluntary workers.

While the grounds were extensively used by inmates, nearby streets were not nearly as accessible since the area was a hilly one. A few people had outdoor transport of their own and the home owned a bus; residents took responsibility for organizing their own activities and the maintenance of the bus. A rota of volunteer drivers could be called on.

The staff, with one exception, did not live in.

The Local Authority Home (LA 1)

This relatively new purpose-built home was also in the suburbs. Material provision was of a very high order. All inmates had either a single room or shared with only one other: in the latter case, the allocation of rooms was as far as possible consistent with personal choice. However, they were discouraged from entertaining visitors in their own rooms.

Public rooms comprised two TV lounges, a writing room cum library, a recreation room, and a dining room. A large attractive hall was again a focal point for interaction between residents and others. The grounds were designed to be accessible to wheelchairs and were frequently used.

Although inmates were free to come and go at any time, they tended to go out in groups in transport that the local authority provided on a regular basis. Only a minority of the residents were able to make use of the nearby shopping centre unaccompanied; for most, the hazards of kerbs and gradients were too great. Members of local churches visited regularly and arranged for transport to and from Sunday services. Community links, however, were relatively weak and voluntary helpers were fewer than in VH 1 and VH 2.

Residents did not participate in decisions on the running of the home, nor, it appeared, did the majority have any wish to do so. Staff, therefore, imposed the rules (for example, that visitors should leave at 8 p.m.) though there was no sense of a rigid discipline.

Apart from the superintendent, who had a flat on the premises, and two or three orderlies, the rest of the staff lived out.

The First RHB Unit (RHB 1)

This unit occupied a converted country mansion. Several large rooms served as wards, each sleeping five or six people. Although considerable efforts had been made to improve the appearance of the wards (by redecorating and by fitting curtains round the beds to give some privacy) there was little provision beyond that of a short-stay hospital. Personal possessions were little in evidence and inmates were not allowed to use the wards as sitting rooms by day. The general appearance was, therefore, much less 'homely' than that of the three institutions described so far.

Public rooms consisted of a large sitting room with television, an occupational therapy room, and a dining room. These were connected by a long corridor. Many of the inmates were dependent on others to move them from one room to another; for that reason there was less movement than in other homes. The majority spent much of the day in the occupational therapy room; others sat in the corridor; while the most helpless patients were wheeled into the sitting room. The grounds, which were extensive, were inaccessible without staff help and were therefore virtually unused by the inmates. In the summer, residents were wheeled out to a courtyard in the centre of the building.

Inmates, in fact, had little or no self-determination. The staff imposed rigid rules. For example, bedtimes were fixed: 7 p.m. for those needing most assistance and 9 p.m. at the latest for the rest.

Transactions with the outside world seemed sparse. Few voluntary workers were involved with the home and inmates seldom went out unless as a group to an activity organized for them by the staff, for example on an outing or to an art class for the disabled.

Many of the nursing and domestic staff lived on the premises.

The Second RHB Unit (RHB 2)

Located in an urban geriatric hospital, this unit comprised a single ward with an adjoining room. Since the ward was not designed for long-stay patients it offered little more provision than short-stay hospitals for personal possessions.

A lift gave access to an occupational therapy room on another floor; but wheelchair-users could not go outside the building without help and there was no garden where inmates might sit out of doors.

A chronic shortage of staff precluded their spending as much time as they thought necessary with inmates. Although a band of voluntary helpers visited twice weekly, arranged entertainments, and took the inmates out on expeditions, additional staff or voluntary helpers might have wheeled inmates up to the main road and to the shopping area. To compensate for this, attempts were made to impose as few restrictions as possible and visitors were, for example, able to call in at any time. The social climate was nevertheless heavy and depressing. There was little communication between individuals, many of whom had speech difficulties, and the 'ward' atmosphere was probably accentuated by the fact that one or two of them were bed-bound, and a few others were put to bed in the late afternoon. (This too was attributed to staff shortages.) There was also a lack of continuity in relationships between inmates and staff, since many of the latter were subject to transfer between this and other wards in the hospital.

COMPARATIVE DATA ON THE INMATES

Age Distribution

Table 1 shows the ages of the inmates in the five institutions. Each of them had come into being to provide for the 'young

TABLE I   *Age of inmates*

| Institution | Years of age | | | | Total |
	Under 21	21-35	36-50	Over 50	
VH 1	0	13	21	5	39
VH 2	0	10	7	4	21
LA 1	6	4	24	13	47
RHB 1	0	2	19	3	24
RHB 2	1	5	6	4	16
Total	7	34	77	29	147

chronic sick' and in two instances the upper age-limit on admission was fixed, at the mid forties and late forties respectively. It may seem surprising, therefore, that more than three-quarters of the inmates were over 35 and only a handful were under 21. In fact, the main requirement for residential care comes from the upper age-groups. This is clear from published data on the younger chronic sick population in RHB establishments (including both ordinary hospital beds and special units). In 1967, 12 per cent of the RHB population were between 15 and 34 (compared with 28 per cent under 35 in our sample); 31 per cent were between 35 and 49 (compared with 52 per cent between 36 and 50); and the remaining 56 per cent were 50-59 (as against 20 per cent in our sample, which included a few who were 60 and over) (source: Ministry of Health, 1968a). Disabled people in the younger age-groups are more likely to be looked after by their families than to seek institutional care; it is in middle age that family resources increasingly break down.

Our data suggest, then, that there is a discrepancy in residential accommodation between the patterns of demand and supply. The under-35s find it relatively easy to get into the specialized institutions – in the two voluntary homes, a third and a half of the inmates respectively were in this age-group – whereas the over-50s appear to obtain much less than their fair share of places even in the special RHB units.

64

Sex Distribution

The data we have (*Table 2*) show a difference between the voluntary and other homes in their provision for the sexes (if we exclude RHB 2, an all-male unit). LA 1 and RHB 1 have a far higher proportion of female residents than have the two voluntary homes, where the sex distribution is almost even. There appears to be a greater demand for residential accommodation for women (and this is supported by the 1968 Ministry of Health circular). Thus the figures for LA 1 and RHB 1 probably reflect the pattern of demand, whereas the two voluntary homes appear to have been pursuing a policy of obtaining a balance between the sexes, regardless of differential need.

TABLE 2   *Sex distribution*

Institution	Male	Female	Total
VH 1	22	17	39
VH 2	9	12	21
LA 1	18	29	47
RHB 1	7	17	24
RHB 2	16	0	16
Total	72	75	147

Age at Onset of Disability

The age an individual has reached when the disability occurs clearly has considerable implications for his life experiences. A severe congenital disability, for example, may prevent a child from attending an ordinary school and in some cases from obtaining an education at all. On the other hand, the individual who becomes affected later in life may have established a career, set up home, and founded a family. In *Table 3* we have chosen 25 as the minimum age at which an individual might fall into this latter category. Another significant age appeared to us to be about 15: below this, the child will not have completed his education; between 15 and 25 the young person may be expected to have left school and started work. Thus an individual who becomes disabled at, say, 18 may have completed his education but have had little experience of a work role and the relative independence that accompanies it.

TABLE 3   *Age at onset of disability*

| Institution | Congenital disability | Years of age | | | Insufficient information | Total |
		Under 15	15-25	Over 25		
VH 1	11	12	6	6	4	39
VH 2	2	10	3	5	1	21
LA 1	17	3	8	18	1	47
RHB 1	1	4	4	9	6	24
RHB 2	5	1	5	5	0	16
Total	36	30	26	43	12	147

From the table it will be seen that 25 per cent of the sample had congenital disabilities, while a further 20 per cent had become disabled during their childhood. Thus 45 per cent of the sample might be expected to have had atypical educational and work experiences. Another 29 per cent had not been affected until they were over 25 years of age.

Table 3 also suggests that the voluntary homes tend to cater more for those who have been crippled in childhood and the RHB units more for those disabled later in life, with the local authority unit falling between the two. This would be consistent with the voluntary homes' bias towards younger applicants for admission.

Education

From *Table 4* it appears that a slightly higher percentage of people than one might have anticipated had completed their ordinary schooling (61 per cent in all). This includes some who were disabled before they were 15, but we cannot tell whether as a result of this they suffered any educational disadvantage.

Almost one-third of the total did not have an ordinary schooling. The majority of these people either went to special schools for the physically handicapped or received spasmodic teaching during periods when they were able to attend elementary schools or when a local authority arranged for a home teacher. Eight had received no formal education. This last figure probably errs on the conservative side since a proportion of those

TABLE 4   *Education*

Institution	Ordinary schooling	Disrupted or special schooling	No formal education	Insufficient information	Total
VH 1	20	13	3	3	39
VH 2	14	6	0	1	21
LA 1	27	16	2	2	47
RHB 1	20	1	0	3	24
RHB 2	8	1	3	4	16
Total	89	37	8	13	147

for whom we have insufficient information had congenital disabilities and severe speech defects.

Work Experience

Table 5 distinguishes those who had held a full-time job and been self-supporting from those who had not. Although a number of inmates earned money from such occupations as handicrafts, painting, typing, and duplicating, none of them acknowledged having an income sufficiently high to pay for their own upkeep. We have therefore excluded them from the self-supporting category, along with those who had attempted to work but had found the demands of the job too great and given up within a few months.

TABLE 5   *Work experience*

Institution	Has been self-supporting	Has not been self-supporting	Insufficient information	Total
VH 1	15	21	3	39
VH 2	12	8	1	21
LA 1	26	19	2	47
RHB 1	15	3	6	24
RHB 2	9	7	0	16
Total	77	58	12	147

By these criteria, just over half of the sample had held down a job, while 40 per cent had never been self-supporting. Of those who had been in full-time employment, however, only thirty-three, or 22 per cent of the total sample, had worked for a period of ten years or more. Taken collectively, therefore, the work experiences of inmates differ more markedly from those of the general population than might at first appear to be the case.

Marital Status

Nearly three-quarters of our sample had never married. The percentage was highest in the two voluntary homes, which, of course, also housed larger numbers of inmates who had been crippled in childhood. A striking feature of *Table 6* is the large proportion of inmates' marriages that had ended in divorce or legal separation.

There is a contrast here with the pattern for disabled adults who have not entered institutions. In one study, nearly half the sample were married, and of those with surviving spouses fewer than 10 per cent were separated or divorced (Townsend, 1967).

TABLE 6   *Marital status*

Institution	Single	Married	Divorced/ separated	Widowed	Total
VH 1	34	0	3	2	39
VH 2	16	2	2	1	21
LA 1	32	3	10	2	47
RHB 1	13	10	1	0	24
RHB 2	10	3	3	0	16
Total	105	18	19	5	147

Experience in Institutions

We shall postpone to a later chapter consideration of the circumstances that lead to admission to institutions. *Table 7* shows that almost half of those we interviewed were in fact already living in an institution before they entered the particular unit where we met them.

TABLE 7   *Residence prior to entry to current institution*

Institution	Own or relative's home	Another institution	Insufficient information	Total
VH 1	19	14	6	39
VH 2	8	12	1	21
LA 1	27	19	1	47
RHB 1	10	8	6	24
RHB 2	5	10	1	16
Total	69	63	15	147

Table 8 sets out the length of time that inmates had spent in institutions. It will be seen that the median period was about five years. Nearly 10 per cent had been continuously in an institution for over twenty years. In some cases the experience of institutional living had begun in childhood: a total of twenty-six inmates had spent periods in hospitals or other institutions under the age of 15; twelve had had experiences of this kind under the age of 5. Periods varied from a few months to several years. Intermittent periods before final admission are not included in the table.

TABLE 8   *Period in institutions*

Institution	Years					Insufficient information	Total
	Less than 1	1-5	6-10	11-20	Over 20		
VH 1	3	4	7	15	5	5	39
VH 2	0	7	5	6	2	1	21
LA 1	6	28	7	3	2	1	47
RHB 1	2	6	6	2	1	7	24
RHB 2	0	4	4	1	3	4	16
Total	11	49	29	27	13	18	147

Distribution of Disabilities

The main disabilities encountered in these five institutions are given in *Table 9*, which shows that three conditions – multiple sclerosis, cerebral palsy, and muscular dystrophy – account for nearly half the total.

Many institutions restrict their intake of people with progressive diseases, since they will sooner or later need increased nursing care. Multiple sclerosis is especially unpopular because of the mental deterioration that sometimes accompanies the later stages. RHB 1 was deviant in its exceptionally high proportion of progressive conditions; RHB 2, on the other hand, diverged in the opposite direction. Thus the distribution of progressive and non-progressive conditions in the two RHB units taken together was not significantly different from their distribution in the other three.

TABLE 9   *Kinds of disability*

Disability	VH 1	VH 2	LA 1	RHB 1	RHB 2	Total
Multiple sclerosis	3	4	9	16	2	34
Cerebral palsy	6	1	8	1	4	20
Muscular dystrophy (& muscular atrophy)	9	2	3	1	1	16
Paralysis *	2	2	4	2	4	14
Osteo & rheumatoid arthritis; Still's disease	5	4	4	0	0	13
Parkinson's disease	1	0	2	2	1	6
Friedreich's ataxia	0	1	3	1	0	5
Poliomyelitis	0	6	0	0	0	6
Dual disabilities	4	0	9	1	1	15
Other	9	1	5	0	3	18
Total	39	21	47	24	16	147

* i.e. hemiplegia, tetraplegia, quadriplegia, paraplegia.

It has to be borne in mind that a progressive condition is not necessarily synonymous with a high level of physical dependency and need for nursing care for the duration of the inmate's stay; there may be periods of several years when the disease remains static. Equally, some inmates with non-progressive diseases may need a great deal of physical care. An individual disabled as a result of polio, for example, may have lost the use of almost all the muscles in his body and be completely dependent on others for every activity.

Tables 10 and *11* illustrate some of the physical effects of the disabilities. It can be seen that nearly 80 per cent of all inmates

TABLE 10   *Impairment of movement: inmates with limbs affected*

	Both upper and lower	Lower only	Upper only	Unaffected	Total
VH 1	27	10	1	1	39
VH 2	20	1	0	0	21
LA 1	34	10	0	3	47
RHB 1	20	4	0	0	24
RHB 2	15	0	1	0	16
Total	116	25	2	4	147

were affected in both upper and lower limbs. However, as we did not obtain a medical assessment of the degree of dis-

TABLE 11   *Percentages of inmates with other impairments* *

	Defective speech	Defective hearing	Defective sight	Incontinence
	%	%	%	%
VH 1	28	8	20	10
VH 2	25	10	15	5
LA 1	49	11	30	13
RHB 1	70	8	29	67
RHB 2	75	0	13	37

* Some inmates had multiple impairments.

ability, *Table 10* does not give a reliable indication of the varying amounts of care required. The percentages of incontinent inmates, shown in *Table 11*, suggest a somewhat greater requirement for care in the two RHB units. These two units also had exceptionally high proportions of people with speech defects; the consequential difficulties of communication inevitably had a dampening effect on social intercourse in these two institutions.

CHAPTER 5

The Tasks and Functions
of Residential Institutions

CHARACTERISTICS OF THE INTAKE

In this chapter we examine certain essential features of residential institutions catering for the physically handicapped and chronic sick and begin to analyse their consequences.

At one level the function of such an institution can be defined quite straightforwardly: it imports cripples and looks after them. But if we are to understand and try to tackle the problems of operating these institutions, it is necessary to be a good deal more precise about what it is that is being imported and the nature of the task that the institution is being called upon to carry out.

Certain aspects of the matter, in so far as they apply to cripples in general, have already been discussed in Chapter 3. Every institution, for example, has to contend with social attitudes towards disability. These not only impinge on the institution from outside, but are imported into it, by managements, by staff, and by the inmates themselves. As we saw, infirmity has psychological – even psychopathological – consequences which are often insidious and even irreversible. If I have a visible handicap, your behaviour towards me will be different in gross or subtle ways from your behaviour towards able-bodied associates; accordingly, my response to you is different from theirs to you; your image of me as different is confirmed; my image of myself is affected by your image of me; thus I am in reality different. The problem of being set apart in this way is one with which every cripple has somehow to cope.

Although inmates of residential institutions are often more physically (and perhaps psychologically) handicapped than those who remain in the community, this is by no means necessarily so. The more critical difference is that they have been rejected. They have for the most part been rejected as individuals, in that their families are no longer willing or able to look after them. More importantly, by crossing the boundary into the institution, whether voluntarily or not, they fall into a rejected category of non-contributors to and non-participants in society, and indeed are virtually non-members of society.

Individual Rejection

Individual experiences of rejection are often blatant. The case of Mrs Atkins is an example:

Mrs Atkins, who is now in her middle fifties, has Parkinson's disease. Her speech is difficult to understand. Two operations have made it possible for her to walk – an awkward, shuffling gait. She easily loses her balance, falls over and bruises herself, and because of this she cannot go out alone. She is able to dress, wash, and bath herself, but it is a painfully slow business: to get dressed takes her about an hour. Her disease began shortly after the birth of her daughter. The first thirteen years of her marriage were spent with her in-laws. Because of her own frail health her mother-in-law brought up the child. By the time Mrs Atkins and her husband were able to afford a home of their own, she was already too incapacitated to manage the housework. She recalled that her husband stayed up until 4 a.m. cleaning the house on their first Christmas in the new home and that he then had to leave at 6 a.m. to go on shift duty. 'He was good to me then.' Subsequently the husband brought another woman into the house; Mrs Atkins was relegated to the spare bedroom. He was violent with her on several occasions and once, when she could no longer cope adequately on her own, left her for three months. Three years ago she saw an article in a local paper describing the institution where she now lives and she herself applied for admission. She later divorced her husband. She showed neither bitterness nor recrimination towards him and could see the strain that was imposed on him by twenty-five years of marriage during which his partner became progressively less able to cope and to provide a normal home life.

73

Plainly, however, his cruelty to her during the last few years was calculated, consciously or not, to drive her away and rid him of an intolerable burden. The daughter is now married with three children of her own and lives only a few miles from the institution. Despite the proximity she apparently visits her mother only about once a year. 'She can't really come with three children.'

Table 6 showed the high rate of divorce or legal separation among inmates. For many of those still classified as married, the status was largely nominal. An exception was Mrs Brown, whose husband moved house to be close to the institution in which she lived: he was able to visit her daily and take her home for a few hours at weekends. Much more often, visits by spouses tend to become increasingly infrequent and perfunctory.[1]

Like Mrs Atkins, many inmates disguise their feeling of rejection and try to cover up:

'He's good to me really but he's busy at weekends.'

But such feelings can be painful. The inmate who commented to the interviewer:

'Matron says we're only here because our relatives won't put up with us'

was perhaps asking to be reassured that her statement was not really true.

Of the inmates who are or have been married, women outnumber men – partly because the caring role is socially defined as a feminine role and this makes it more appropriate for a wife to look after a disabled husband than vice versa. This is reinforced by the structure of financial aid. The disabled husband normally has some kind of pension which makes it at least possible, if difficult, for the wife to devote her time to looking after him without having to take up other employment. No corresponding financial help is available if it is the wife who is disabled. Unless, therefore, the husband's financial

[1] Other studies have confirmed the strong inverse correlation between length of stay in an institution and frequency of visits (e.g. Wing, 1962).

resources are substantial, he cannot arrange for someone to look after his wife at home. It is then difficult to find any alternative to an institution.

The married inmates are, of course, for the most part those who have been disabled only later in life. Those who have been crippled at birth or in childhood are much less likely ever to get married. They have usually experienced a lifetime of successive rejections.

As a child of 7 Mr Collins had a disease which caused a great deal of pain, hampered his growth, and led to a weakened heart. He stopped going to school and his life from then on was confined to a series of hospitals, where he received little tuition. He claims that he taught himself to read. His deprivation was intensified by a permanent rift between his parents. His mother, he felt, wanted nothing to do with him; his father could not cope alone; so he stayed in hospital until he was moved to the home where we met him. His father had continued to visit him until his death some years previously; his mother never contacted him.

In other cases, lengthy periods of hospitalization have been accompanied by strongly supportive parental relationships.

Miss Davies, for example, who has Still's disease, is one of a family of five children. She spent most of the first nine years of her life in a leading orthopaedic hospital, which she entered at 18 months. Diagnoses in the early days were uncertain. Towards the end of the stay in hospital there was a suggestion that her legs should be amputated below the knee since it was thought that she would never be able to walk, but her mother would not agree to the operation and she was discharged. Her memory of the years in hospital is vague. At 10 she went to school for the first time. This was a primary school for normal children. At first the school had refused to take her on the ground that the responsibility for a crippled child was too great; but her mother was determined that she should go to an ordinary school rather than to a special school and successfully appealed to her Member of Parliament. Miss Davies feels that it was due to her mother's

75

determination that she learnt to walk. Despite her prolonged stay in the orthopaedic hospital she had been unable to walk when she left. The local GP's advice was to keep her moving as much as possible and her mother insisted that she practised walking daily around the garden. If she fell, she had to pick herself up. Now, at the age of 30, she has had to come into an institution because she is also going blind. In view of this second disability she thinks it particularly fortunate that her mother did not agree to the amputation.

It is important to recognize that although in retrospect Miss Davies's mother can be seen rationally to have been supportive and helpful, the child's subjective experience was nevertheless one of rejection by her mother. Whatever the compelling reasons, the mother did not look after her, but sent her away. This deprivation of the child's normal experience of reliable mothering is common among those who are hospitalized in infancy or early childhood.

Social Rejection

So far we have been considering manifestations of personal rejection, which, to a greater or lesser degree, has been experienced by almost every inmate coming into an institution of this kind. This will obviously have psychological effects on them as individuals and thus on the relationship they make with the institution. The second type of rejection we mentioned was social rejection – the rejection of inmates as non-contributors to and non-participants in society. While this will also be experienced by inmates individually in various ways and will often be bound up with personal rejection, we are more concerned here with its impact on inmates as a category and thus on the relation between all institutions of this type and the society that has exported them.

The cripple who has not been put into an institution clings on, albeit often precariously, to some kind of status within the wider society. Least socially handicapped is the cripple who is not only in work but is also a breadwinner. The roles conferred by his job and by his position in the family override his status as a cripple: he thus approximates to a 'normal' member of society.

Jobs, however, are more difficult to find for cripples than for the able-bodied and, once obtained, more difficult to hold.[1] However irrelevant it may be to the individual's work capacity, the disability almost always obtrudes into the relationship between employer and employee. Cripples frequently report peremptory dismissals without explanation. Whether they are in reality victimized is, of course, impossible to ascertain; nevertheless, the feeling of victimization is real and inevitably colours the relationship with the next prospective employer. The cripple is suspicious and distrustful of the employer's motives; aware of this, the employer is himself on guard; and the outcome is all too predictable.

One should perhaps be surprised that more cripples do not give up the struggle and seek some kind of sanctuary. Giving up the struggle, however, also means giving up the social status that goes with the job. Although to most of us this may not seem a social status that confers a great many privileges, the lack of it certainly carries with it major deprivations.

Rehabilitation was defined for us by the head of one rehabilitation unit in terms of acquiring the status of a tax-payer. This reflects the value that our society assigns to work. Society both applies pressure on every child to assume this status and invests substantial resources in educational and therapeutic institutions whose task is to prepare people for this status or to restore them to it. In some cases these resources seem not to have been deployed as effectively as they might have been.

Mr Edwards, now 53, is an example. He contracted polio as an infant. He has no movement below the waist and his right arm and hand are completely useless. He can just manage to store a cigarette between two fingers on his right hand, but cannot move the hand. His left arm, too, has very little movement but his left hand is extremely good. This is his principal asset. He was kept at home for a few years as a child but spent most of his life in hospitals or institutions. His

[1] Townsend (1967) asserts that some employers abuse the Disabled Persons (Employment) Act 'by persuading some lightly handicapped persons . . . to register as disabled . . .' Others, he maintains, pay low wages.

parents died when he was in his late teens and although he
has a number of brothers and sisters they don't want to know
him. He had been at a hospital fairly near his home in Kent
until the war broke out, when he was evacuated to Lanca-
shire. He stayed in a hospital there throughout the war.
(This distance from home made it almost inevitable that he
would be cut off from family and relatives.) Shortly after
the war he was transferred to yet another hospital in the
south. From there he was sent for a twelve-week period to a
rehabilitation centre, the object being to assess his capacity
for work. Because of his chequered history of hospitalization
he had received only two years of schooling; such proficiency
as he had in reading and writing was largely self-taught. To
assess his capacity he was given a number of tests which he
passed fairly well. He was told that he was fit to hold down a
job. He was also told, however, that it was up to him to
get a job to hold down. That was out of the question, so he
returned to hospital. Somewhat later a welfare worker suggested that he should go in for book-keeping. Various half-
promises were made but nothing came of it. Subsequently
a surgeon suggested that he should have his useless right
hand amputated and replaced by an artificial hand which
would enable him to do a little more. Again, nothing came of
this. Finally, he got himself transferred from hospital to the
residential institution where he now lives. This is a place
that offers him a much more benign environment and also
relative security of tenure. After he had been there for two
years the notion of his taking up book-keeping was raised
again and it was suggested that he be transferred to another
establishment which specializes in retraining the physically
handicapped. How far these previous episodes had come to
nothing because of his own reluctance is impossible to tell.
He himself says that he was not enthusiastic about having
his hand amputated but he was willing. By the time this final
proposal to take up book-keeping was made, however, he
certainly felt that he had had enough. He understood that if
he failed the proposed training course there was no guarantee
that he would be able to come back to the institution he was

in and if he passed there was similarly no guarantee about where he might be transferred. He therefore elected to stay where he was.

However one may apportion responsibility for the outcome between Mr Edwards and his rehabilitators, the fact is that rehabilitation, though evidently regarded by both as the desirable objective, remained a chimera. In this respect, his case is not atypical of the reported experience of a great many in these institutions. Their lives before they were institutionalized have been a succession of hopes raised and hopes dashed. By external criteria they have failed.

The sense of failure seems particularly strong in those who as children have been to special residential schools for physically handicapped and have received along with their education and training the impression that when they grow up they will be able to find employment and take their place in society. Others, as children, have no doubt been buoyed up through a series of difficult and painful operations by the hope, explicit or implied, that the next operation would bring recovery or at least an improvement in functioning; and, too often, it has not done so. Work, and the status that goes with it, is highly important as an aspiration.

The cripple who cannot work and is supported by parents or by a spouse feels deprived and the deprivation extends to other members of the family. From time to time the plight of these families is publicized in the press: for example, the husband who is trying to hold down a full-time job and also look after his incurably ill wife. But what is important is that the deprivation is shared; and the dependent cripple (even a Mrs Atkins) still retains a vicarious social status as a member of a family which has a place in society. The husband just referred to asked through the columns of the newspaper whether he should give up his job so as to devote his full attention to his wife. Readers earnestly advised him not to, on the very real grounds that by doing so he would be further attenuating his wife's vicarious link with the social world outside.

For inmates in a residential institution even this vicarious link has been severed.

79

CONSEQUENCES FOR THE PRIMARY TASK

This examination of some characteristics of the 'human through-put' enables us to define more rigorously the task of these residential institutions and to see in what respects they differ from other residential institutions that superficially seem comparable.

Physical handicap by itself is not the discriminating factor; nor is the experience of personal rejection. More critical is the fact that when people cross the boundary into such an institution they are displaying that they have failed to occupy or retain any role which, according to the norms of society, confers social status on the individual. Even in this respect, however, the crippled inmate is comparable with the convict committed to prison or the patient committed to a psychiatric hospital. What is significantly different is that the prison and, nowadays, the psychiatric hospital sooner or later discharge almost all their inmates and have grounds for hoping that some will be reformed or cured and take up socially valued roles in the outside world. By contrast the boundary of the kind of institution we are discussing is, by and large, a point of no return. It is exceptional indeed for an inmate to be restored to some semblance of a normal role in the wider society. Usually he will remain in the institution, or in another of the same category, until he dies.

To lack any actual or potential role that confers a positive social status in the wider society is tantamount to being socially dead. To be admitted to one of these institutions is to enter a kind of limbo in which one has been written off as a member of society but is not yet physically dead.

In these terms, the task that society assigns – behaviourally though never verbally – to these institutions is to cater for the socially dead during the interval between social death and physical death.

COMPENSATORY VALUES

A few inmates recognize this implicit definition of the task of the institution. It is a receptacle for those who are beyond salvage – 'the scrapheap of human rejects' (Brown, 1966, p. 140). In January 1968, when the 'Back Britain' movement was sweeping the country, a macabre joke was going about in one institution: 'Let's back Britain', it was suggested, 'by all committing suicide. We could save the country £30,000 a year.'

If one is in a situation of hopeless adversity, cynicism is one form of defence. No doubt some of the inmates who refer to themselves as being on 'the scrapheap of human rejects' are half hoping to be contradicted – and they usually are. An able-bodied commentator who makes a remark to this effect is liable to arouse angry protest. Indeed, although there may be some inmates who, however reluctantly, see the reality of the situation they are in, the majority of inmates and almost all staff and members of the wider society find the notion of the social death sentence altogether too painful to contemplate.

Both the widespread use of the specialized 'limbo' institutions and the attitudes towards them are the result of three features of contemporary society. First, medical advances designed to prolong life have often succeeded merely in postponing death; second, the diminished size of the family unit has reduced its viability in holding its sick or ageing members; and third, the declining force of the values and rituals of Christianity has left society without any adequate cultural mechanisms for coping with death.

The last point is particularly important. As Geoffrey Gorer (1965) and others have pointed out, death in contemporary society has come to be looked upon as obscene. In contrast to, for example, the Indian joint family, where the growing child experiences the cycle of birth and death as being almost as natural as the cycle of the seasons and the crops, in our own society many adults have yet to see their first corpse. The idea of death – the death of others and, more particularly, the death of oneself – is shut away. We lack socially sanctioned devices to express our grief and share our work of mourning. To die or to be bereaved is to commit a social gaffe and, as with social gaffes of other kinds, the recommended procedure is: 'Least said, soonest mended.'

The cripple, of course – especially the victim of an incurable and progressive disease – is an ugly reminder of mortality. It is perhaps for this reason that we are particularly prone in contemporary society to put these rejects out of sight in special institutions of their own. By the same token, the reality of what is being done must also be denied.

Since it is too painful to acknowledge explicitly what society is implicitly asking these institutions to do, two sets of values are commonly brought into use as defence mechanisms. These may be labelled the humanitarian or medical value that prolongation of life is a good thing and the liberal or anti-medical value that the handicapped inmates of these institutions are 'really normal'.

The Humanitarian Defence

Although the social death sentence has been passed, the pressure of humanitarian values is to keep the interval between social and physical death as long as possible. The medical profession is one of the carriers of these values on behalf of society. Doctors and nurses are committed to preserving and prolonging life without asking for what purpose. Not long ago there was a public outcry in Britain when it was disclosed that a hospital consultant had issued written instructions that resuscitation procedures were not to be applied in cases of heart failure if the victims were over the age of 70. If doctors exercise any discretion of this kind, they are expected to do so quietly and discreetly. When the demand for life-saving apparatus, such as kidney machines, outstrips supply we give the medical profession no guidance as to whose lives to save and whose to sacrifice. This is a painful reality that we prefer not to discuss and by and large the medical profession colludes with the rest of society in this respect.

In a hospital ward set aside for the 'young chronic sick' we saw a young man who had suffered brain damage through oxygen starvation during a heart operation. His body was largely paralysed, he had no speech, and he showed no signs of awareness of what was going on around him. He frequently screamed and occasionally tried to attack the nurses. When

82

we asked the specialist whether he didn't think that both the patient and his family might be better off if he were dead, the specialist was indignant. It was his job, he said, to preserve life 'and we must never forget that in another ten years there may be a cure for this'. Later he acknowledged the conflict he felt when faced with such cases.

While humanitarian values apply pressure to postpone physical death for as long as possible there is reluctance to acknowledge the unhappiness and lack of fulfilment of many of the lives that are so prolonged. Society wants to believe that the inmates are happy and contented and demands that they behave as if they were happy and contented. We heard of one institution where the chairman of the Management Committee would stride in breezily every morning and say:

'Oh what a happy place this is! It always gives me such pleasure to come here.'

As one inmate commented:

'How can we tell her what we really feel like?'

For the inmate to show discontent is to show ingratitude and this is an affront to humanitarian values.

The Liberal Defence

In this respect, superficially at least, the liberal value is at variance with the humanitarian. The abnormality of the inmates is denied: it is claimed that they are 'really normal'. It is the liberal conviction that the institutionalized cripple ought to be accepted by the rest of society and it is implied that if he develops the capacities remaining to him he will in fact be accepted. Hopes of physical and, more particularly, social rehabilitation are thus encouraged.

However, any inmate who takes too literally the liberal protestations that he is really normal, and who behaves accordingly by trying to cross back to the other side of the boundary, quickly discovers his mistake. The encouragement given to an aspiring foot- or mouth-painter tends to be in inverse proportion to the income that his paintings produce: if his income as an inmate approaches income levels in the world outside he becomes an awkward anomaly in the system.

Earlier we described the case of Mr Edwards, who refused to risk the uncertainties of giving up his place in an institution for the doubtful fruits of a course in book-keeping. He nevertheless did not stagnate. Exploiting the dexterity of his good left hand, he began to manufacture costume jewellery and took samples of this to a department store where one of the buyers said that they would sell as much as he could provide. He could not work very fast but over a period of about eighteen months began to build a modest business, clearing a total of some £40 after his materials had been paid for. At the end of this period he received a visit from a Customs and Excise official who said that he understood that he had been selling jewellery. Mr Edwards was required to show the official his receipts and it was pointed out to him that under the purchase-tax regulations he was obliged to pay 50 per cent of his takings to Customs and Excise. They agreed to waive any tax due on the work he had done already but told him not to undertake any more unless he was prepared to pay the purchase tax. Mr Edwards concluded that if he put his prices up to a level that would still give him some profit margin, he would price himself out of the market. He therefore gave up making costume jewellery. Nowadays he is still active in the workshop of his institution and satisfies his entrepreneurial drives by being the institution's tobacco and cigarette merchant. He buys these at wholesale prices and gives 50 per cent of his profits to the institution's welfare fund.

Like others receiving social security benefits, a handicapped person has his allowance cut if his earnings exceed £2. 1s. per week. Similarly, the inmate whose upkeep in an institution is paid for by a local authority ceases to be eligible for support if he is gainfully employed – even though there may be an unbridgeable gap between what he earns and what he would need to support himself. This is reminiscent of trade union protests against prison inmates being allowed to earn money from real work in contrast to the make-work of sewing mail-bags. The inmate must not compete with normals. Society is curiously intolerant of the half and half, of the uncategorizable.

Staff who profess liberal values frequently proceed to infantilize inmates by claiming, for example, that their home is 'one big happy family'. The analogy is clear: they identify the inmates with children and themselves with parents. Their assertion that they believe inmates are 'really normal' is all too often belied by some disparaging remark: for instance,

'I think it's good for them to have boyfriends but of course [with a laugh] their little affairs don't last very long.'

TWO MODELS OF RESIDENTIAL CARE

Associated with these two values, the humanitarian and the liberal, we have identified two models of residential care which we call here the Warehousing Model and the Horticultural Model. These define the primary task of a residential institution in rather different ways.

The Warehousing Model

In the warehousing model, the primary task becomes: to prolong physical life. It represents an attempt to translate the model of the hospital into the setting of the residential institution. The intake into the system is a patient defined in terms of physical malfunctioning. The conversion process entails the provision of medical and nursing care. This provision is facilitated if the inmate, as the object of these ministrations, accepts his dependent role in the system. Acceptance of temporary dependency is functional in the hospital setting as a means to an end: the output, it is hoped, is a person restored to his normal roles in the world outside. Doctors and nurses derive satisfaction from their contribution to this process. Institutions for incurables, however, can provide neither the hope for the patients nor the conventional satisfaction for staff. In the hospital, the patient who dies, however inevitable his death may be, is the failure of a process directed towards cure; in the institution, there are no cures: the only outputs are dead patients. Medical and nursing skills are thus redirected from the familiar task of curing to the task of postponing death.

We discuss in a later chapter the problems for both parties of providing and receiving intimate physical services. Both the anxieties of the ordinary hospital situation and the defences used to cope with them are magnified in the long-stay institution. One common defence that may be mentioned here is the depersonalization of patients into 'cases'.

> When one of us visited a special ward set aside for young chronic sick within a larger hospital, the consultant in charge, despite our protestations that our interest and qualifications were non-medical, proudly showed off each patient in turn, describing his condition, treatment, and prognosis. In one case – a woman crippled with arthritis, compelled to lie permanently on her back – the consultant had a screen put round the bed, raised the woman's nightdress to her thighs and, with something of the pride of a philatelist displaying a rare stamp, drew detailed attention to her deformed and twisted legs. In this ward the performance of the primary task that the warehousing model implies could hardly have been surpassed. One cannot but be reminded, however, of the efforts made in prison to prevent the convicted murderer from dying in any other way than through judicial execution.

To the extent that effective performance of the warehousing task requires the inmate to remain dependent and depersonalized, any attempts by the inmate to assert himself, or to display individual needs other than those arising from his specific disability, are in the warehousing model constraints on task performance. They are therefore to be discouraged. The 'good' inmate is one who accepts the staff's diagnosis of his needs and the treatment they prescribe and administer.

The Horticultural Model

In the horticultural model, by contrast, it is needs for physical care that are the constraints. The intake into the system is conceived as a deprived individual with unsatisfied drives and unfulfilled capacities. The primary task is to develop these capacities. Thus the conversion process is concerned with providing encouragement for the individual development of inmates in the direction of greater independence – in complete contrast to the dependency orientation inherent in the warehousing model. The role of staff that follows from this horticultural ideology is thus not to treat the disability but to provide opportunities for the growth of abilities.

The horticultural model is a relatively recent development. The warehousing model represents the conventional approach to residential care and is still to be found in relatively pure form, especially in some medically based institutions that are as yet only slightly tempered by what we describe here as liberal values. The horticultural model, on the other hand, is less likely to be found in a pure form – it is an aspiration rather than a reality – and in some institutions the two models coexist somewhat uncomfortably together.

THE MODELS AS SOCIAL DEFENCE MECHANISMS

We shall be saying more about the operation of these two models in the chapters that follow. Here, however, we wish to draw attention to the use of these models as defence mechanisms.

In order to look at them in this way it is necessary to try to break out of the straitjacket of one's own value system. We ourselves, when we embarked upon this study, were very much caught up with the liberal values of the horticultural model. We were captured by the plight of intelligent cripples in particular who were forced to lead stunted lives in institutions that did not provide opportunities for their development. We were antipathetic to the warehousing ideology. There seemed to be no point in prolonging physical existence for its own sake and we would argue that individuals should be given a greater opportunity to determine their own lives and to take risks, even if this might mean shortening their life-span – though it was comforting to believe that, despite the risks, the fuller and richer life that the horticultural model offered might actually postpone death rather than hasten it.

It is not difficult to recognize the inadequacies of a warehousing system in which inmates are treated as helpless bodies to be processed – to be got out of bed, washed, dressed, fed, put on the lavatory, entertained, and kept busy. If emotional and psychological needs are denied or discounted, the most expert and devoted care of the body can destroy the person. The system all too readily projects into the patients its own image of their helplessness, which then pervades their whole life.

It is less easy to see that the horticultural model is also inadequate. The philosophy that people are more than their disabilities and the emphasis on development of individual capacities seem unexceptionable. Yet paradoxically this approach may deprive at least some individuals of their real needs. The pressure to maintain or increase independence may be inappropriate and even distressing to someone with multiple sclerosis or muscular dystrophy who, as his disease progresses, faces a gradual or stepwise decline. Acceptance of dependency may fit the needs of some much better than the struggle against it. Thus the declining multiple sclerotic may feel just as deprived in the horticultural climate as the lively youngster with polio in a warehousing culture that is geared to brain-damaged 'vegetables'.

Few inmates, therefore, fit either model entirely. The same individual may feel somewhat more comfortable with one model in the earlier stages of his institutionalization and with the other model later. We argue that the models cannot be adequate because the tasks they represent are not real tasks. They are essentially social defence mechanisms set up to cope with the intolerable anxieties that are associated with the task that society implicitly defines for these institutions. Like other social defence mechanisms, they are obviously, in part, functional. They support individual defences both of the inmates and of the people who look after them. They also support the defences of members of the wider society who are, however occasionally, reminded of the existence of these institutions. As with other defence mechanisms, however, they have a dysfunctional component as well.

What both models neglect and deny is that, if we are correct in our interpretation that by the very fact of committing people to institutions of this type, society is defining them as, in effect, socially dead, then the essential task to be carried out is to help the inmates to make their transition from social death to physical death. Denial of the meaning of this boundary between the institution and the wider society, between the 'dead' and the living, can lead (as we saw, for example, in Chapter 2) to splitting within the institution between staff and residents or between one group of staff and another, and also to processes of canonization and scapegoating.

What is most intolerable about the real task as we define it here is that it might imply that the individual himself could have a choice about when to die. Paradoxically this is still regarded as an affront to society, even though society has effectively washed its hands of the inmates as significant social beings. Pressed to its logical conclusion, the real task would imply that the inmate on entering such an institution could be given a capsule that would bring about instantaneous and painless death whenever he chose to take it. Such logic, of course, transgresses too many deep-seated cultural values: even to suggest such a possibility would be regarded as outrageous.

Yet so long as the unthinkableness of this alternative persists and is in effect repressed and denied by the substitute tasks derived from the humanitarian and liberal values, it may also become impossible to contemplate more appropriate approaches to the processes of residential care in institutions of this kind. Perhaps we are too guilty about the social death sentence (that behaviourally we have passed and verbally deny) and we fear that if they are given the opportunity of electing when to die the inmates will affront us by swallowing the capsule forthwith. It may be salutary to recall the well-known story of the judge who passed sentence of death on a prisoner but showed clemency by allowing him to choose the manner of his death. The prisoner's retort was immediate: 'I'd like to die of old age, sir.' The corollary of recognizing that the social death sentence has already been passed and that the individual may be left with the choice of when and how to die is the recognition of the individual's right to determine how he would like to spend

89

the intervening period. This includes the right to choose dependency, or to take advantage of developmental opportunities. It then becomes the task of the institution first to help the individual to make his decision and second to provide him with the facilities to implement it.

This definition of the task challenges the warehousing assumption and defence that inmates have only physical needs. It also challenges the horticultural assumption and defence that they are 'really normal'. It demands recognition that, while on the one hand inmates have in common the experience of having been extruded from the wider society and of no longer being able to aspire to its norms of achievement, they are at the same time widely diverse individuals with diverse and changing needs. It implies that it is the task of the institution, without either destroying the inmate's individuality or denying his dependence, to provide a setting in which he can find his own best way of relating to the external world and to himself.

We attempt in Part II to identify more clearly the conditions necessary for performing this task and the obstacles that stand in the way of achieving it.

Processes of
Residential Care

CHAPTER 6

The Import Process

In Chapter 5 we discussed in general terms the characteristics of the inmates and the consequences for the institutions catering for them. Here we focus more specifically on the processes through which the institutions acquire their intake. The dialogue that occurs between an institution and the sources of its intake during the procedure for accepting and rejecting candidates provides interesting evidence of the discrepancies between the institution's definition of its task and the functions it is being called upon by society to fulfil.

Every enterprise must, of course, exercise some control over its intakes. Definition of the primary task determines the characteristics of the intake and of the resources required to process it. Changes in the intake are likely to reduce the effectiveness of task performance; or alternatively they may lead to a redefinition of the primary task and thus of the resources required.

In the first part of this chapter we describe the admission procedures in the five institutions we studied. On the basis of data from these and other institutions we then comment on some of the issues raised – in particular, on the way in which the criteria and methods of selection provide defence mechanisms for those responsible for selection. Finally we examine some differences between inmates as regards their experience of crossing the boundary into the institution.

ADMISSION PROCEDURES

VH 1

The constitution of this voluntary home prescribes that the young chronic sick for whom it is intended should be

'willing to work in as far as their capacity permits and should be of such intelligence and ability as to benefit from the special facilities and atmosphere of the home'.

While such a description is sufficiently general to give rise to a variety of interpretations by different people, it does seem to exclude those in the terminal stages of a progressive disease; or, more correctly, it precludes the institution's being largely given over to such cases. A question that those responsible for admissions have always to ask is what the potential inmate can offer to the life of the community. It could presumably be argued that even the most severely disabled individual has something to offer, if it is only to give other inmates the opportunity to be of some service to him. However, this institution limits its intake of heavy-nursing cases in view of its constitution and of the proportion of existing inmates who will ultimately require heavy nursing.

Emphasis on a community or family spirit is reflected in the admission procedure. This gives a prospective inmate an opportunity to choose whether or not he wishes to settle in the institution besides giving existing inmates and staff an opportunity to decide whether the applicant will prove compatible.

The selection process is divided into four stages. First, the medical and other records of applicants or referrals are screened. Second, those who survive the screening are invited to spend an 'assessment holiday' of about two weeks at the institution. (Sometimes these stages are reversed and a visitor occupying a holiday bed decides that he would like to apply for permanent admission.) Suitable candidates are transferred to a deferred waiting-list. They are not, however, given a firm promise that they will ultimately receive a place. Third, when a vacancy arises, a short list is prepared. Here additional criteria come into play: for example, sex (if the place is in a shared room) or source of support (if it is an RHB contractual bed that is vacant). This is also an occasion for weeding out from the deferred list some of those who have meanwhile found other accommodation, died, or deteriorated too much to be eligible. The final stage is selection from the short list.

The interval between application and admission ranges from a few months to as long as four years. There may, for example, be delay in offering a holiday bed. At the time of our study, beds were not kept specifically for this purpose, but

94

were available only when existing inmates went on holiday or temporarily to hospital. Or an applicant may not be able to accept a holiday vacancy at short notice. Again, the home situation of a short-listed candidate may have improved, so that he wishes to postpone transfer from the deferred list.

The Management Committee, which is formally responsible for running the institution, delegates control over admissions to a subcommittee. This is chaired by the RHB consultant to the institution – who, organizationally, is an outsider – and comprises representatives of Management Committee, the institution's medical officer (an *ex-officio* member of Management Committee), the warden, and the matron (these being full-time employees of the institution). In practice, the first two stages of the admission process, up to inclusion on the deferred waiting-list, are delegated to the latter three members of the subcommittee. It is noticeable that these three, who have had personal contact with the candidates and are thus alive to their needs, find it difficult to argue against their selection on the basis of need. Other members of the subcommittee who have not met the candidates personally are more in a position to inquire whether they would also be able to contribute to the community. The decision to accept or reject is, however, a joint one. Existing inmates are free, and indeed encouraged, to make known their views informally to staff or outside members of the subcommittee, but the practice of including inmate representatives in an advisory capacity was discontinued some years ago. The Management Committee gave as its reasons an over-preoccupation among inmates with the criteria of capacity and an insufficient concern for criteria of need.

VH 2

Here too the Management Committee appoints a subcommittee to deal with admissions. Applications for admission are passed in the first instance to a medical adviser who decides whether the applicants appear to be potentially suitable for the home. He is mainly concerned with the degree of physical impairment: since the home was set up to cater for the active young chronic sick, applicants who are bedridden or shortly likely to become

95

so are considered unsuitable. The heavily disabled who may be able, with the aid of gadgets, to achieve a measure of independence within the home are not precluded. Those who are rejected at this stage are informed; others are told that their application will be considered when a vacancy arises.

Before anyone can be accepted into the home he must spend a fortnight's assessment holiday there. The matron will then decide whether or not he would meet the community criteria of acceptability, which are intelligence and, to some extent, social background. Although the home did not set out to cater for any particular level of intelligence (though mental defectiveness was barred) or social class, the proportion of inmates with a professional background is higher than in most other institutions. Too wide a discrepancy between newcomers and the inmate community is felt to be fair to neither. There is no particular age-limit – 'their mental and physical state and outlook on life are more important than age' – but applicants over 50 tend to be viewed less favourably. People with a history of mental illness are not likely to be accepted.

When a vacancy occurs the subcommittee considers those applicants who, having spent a holiday at the home, are still regarded as suitable. In this way the final responsibility is again shared.

LA 1

Although this unit is administered by one local authority, it receives finance and inmates from several others. This feature of its situation has had a significant effect on the admission process and thus on the nature of the institution. It has meant that each authority has a quota of beds on which it has first call. And, more importantly, the task of the institution has tended to be slightly but significantly redefined in the direction of dealing with the problems of the local authorities, who are the clients, rather than with the needs of the inmates as such.

LA 1 was originally intended to provide hostel accommodation for younger handicapped people still at work and sheltered employment both for other less capable inmates and for cripples living at home. When it first opened, admission was carefully controlled. Candidates were jointly assessed by the head of the unit and an officer of the local authority's Welfare Department; and in addition they were required to spend a trial weekend in residence. This did not last. Although it had been expected that the new purpose-built institution would attract people out of squalid home environments, it failed to do so in sufficient numbers. Beds remained empty and the contributing authorities felt under pressure to fill them in order to justify the cost of building the establishment.

Now there is no unified policy or responsibility for admission. The head of the unit is no longer involved to the same extent in assessment. Referrals come instead from local welfare officers. Sometimes potential inmates pay a brief preliminary visit to the institution – to allow them to see whether it will suit them rather than vice versa – while at other times the unit is simply notified of their impending arrival. The quota arrangement and the corresponding dispersal of responsibility reduce the possibility of argument between the authority that operates the unit and the others that use it. There is no institutional waiting-list, though there may be decentralized lists maintained by the respective authorities. Thus the head of the unit who will have to live with the result of other people's decisions has no real power to exercise a veto; nor has the Welfare Department of the administering authority in the face of a claim by another authority.

As a result, although the population of LA 1 has a distribution of physical disabilities broadly similar to that in the other homes – at the one extreme, a handful still capable of outside employment; at the other, several in the terminal stages of multiple sclerosis – there is a higher incidence of emotional disorders, often the outcome of severe deprivation. It seems probable that acute or long-standing social and domestic problems attract the attention of local welfare officers, who then see the institution on their own doorstep as offering a ready solution.

It appears that a certain amount of selection occurs, however, after the inmate has been in the institution for some time. For example, a woman who was allegedly suffering from multiple sclerosis showed signs of emotional disturbance but few symptoms of the disease as such. After she had been in the institution for two or three years, the head of the unit sent her to a specialist. When it was found that she was in fact not suffering from multiple sclerosis or any physical disability, the matter was discussed with her and arrangements were made for her to move out into council accommodation. She was allowed a considerable length of time to come to terms with this idea and was encouraged to take up some part-time employment outside in the meantime. A few others, too, were assisted to move out after they had been in the institution for some time and felt that they would be able to cope with a flat of their own. Again they were assisted by the local authority, which provided them with accommodation.

RHB 1

Responsibility for assessing prospective inmates is vested in the RHB consultant, who is aided by a medical social worker. Although the consultant exercises general supervision over the unit, a variety of other duties take up most of his time. The matron, who is the effective head of the unit, plays no part in the admission procedure; nor does the local Hospital Management Committee have any say in it.

Assessment is subject to powerful and conflicting pressures. More than half of those referred are still living at home in deteriorating circumstances, and the consultant in his domiciliary visit is caught up in the complex and painful problems of the family and the individual concerned, relating to rejecting and being rejected. In some instances the cripple has not been told the purpose of the visit: here the consultant refuses to take over the family's task of disclosing to the individual that they wish to put him into an institution. In others, a person with a progressive disease does not realize the extent to which he will ultimately become disabled and resists the idea of entering an institution. Sometimes the home situation has already broken down completely by the time the case is referred: one husband, for example, refused to take his wife back after she had to spend a short time in hospital; he threatened to leave with the children if she were returned home. Or again, a progressive illness may already be so far advanced that the family is no longer capable of giving the necessary care.

In relation to the demands, the consultant's resources are slender. There is only the one RHB unit for disabled to which he can send them. He has a lien on beds in some four voluntary homes which have contractual arrangements with the RHB, but they impose admission criteria of their own and will not necessarily take the cases that the consultant deems most needy or urgent. The only alternatives open to him are a geriatric unit, which he regards as unsuitable – indeed, it was because of its unsuitability that this special unit for the young chronic sick was established – and the local general hospital, where the physician-in-charge would probably refuse admission; 'so they are left to die at home of bed-sores'.

The aim of the unit when it first started in the late 1950s was to provide a community for young chronic sick who were mentally alert enough to make a contribution to it. Accordingly the upper age-limit for admission was set at 45. Despite the fact that most people in need of residential care were between 45 and 60 (over which age, of course, they qualified for admission to a geriatric unit), the consultant and his predecessors had managed to retain the age-limit. But with the pressures to accept a high proportion of people in the advanced stages of multiple sclerosis and other progressive illnesses, the criterion of mental alertness had been whittled down. The consultant believed the lack of alternative facilities for advanced cases made this outcome inevitable:

> 'We are a last resort. The voluntary homes can skim the cream and pick and choose.'

A waiting-list is maintained and at the time of the study the interval between acceptance and admission was about eighteen months. In the consultant's opinion this was completely unrealistic, since many on the waiting-list managed to find alternative accommodation in the meantime, or else died. The RHB, he said, was nevertheless obliged to keep the waiting-list 'as a sop to public opinion'.

RHB 2

Admission to this unit was controlled by its consultant, who was also physician-in-charge of the hospital of which the unit is a part. His intake came mainly from other hospitals.

He did not adopt stringent criteria. Although RHB 2 was intended for patients between 15 and 59, he did not always adhere to the upper age-limit. The principal constraint was the availability of nursing staff. For example, he might have to defer the admission of a brain-damaged patient still requiring intensive nursing care. But provided he had a vacant bed and sufficient staff, he would accept the patients that other hospitals offered. In contrast to other units, this ward had one or two vacancies during the period of the study.

As in LA 1, a certain amount of selection appeared to occur after admission. Records showed that some patients stayed for periods of only a few days. These were usually people who left on finding conditions uncongenial to them. In some instances the 'host' community had plainly rejected the new arrival. The consultant could discern no apparent reasons for either acceptance or rejection; but when rejection occurred, he arranged a transfer. The consultant himself regarded voluntary homes as more suitable than his own unit for many long-stay patients and whenever possible he encouraged inmates to move to a voluntary home. There appeared to be two main features governing length of stay: first, that inmates were within easy reach of relatives; second, that they were not suited for transfer to a voluntary home.

PROBLEMS OF SELECTION AND REJECTION

Admission procedures are not only the means through which the manifest task of selection is carried out; they also have the function of providing the selectors with a form of defence against the problems of rejection. Institutions catering for the needy are in a sellers' market: by accepting one 'customer' they are explicitly or implicitly rejecting others who are just as needy, if not more so. Rejection may lead to the breakdown of a family which has hitherto just been managing, or to premature death.

This applies particularly to institutions striving to operate a horticultural model. All the pressures from society are to extrude its most helpless members, while the institution is assessing them in terms of the potential development of their remaining capacities. The more rigorous it is in rejecting those who do not fit its specifications, the more benign the setting it is likely to be able to provide for those it selects; but the appropriate balance between criteria of need and of remaining capacity is difficult to maintain. Correspondingly, more elaborate admission procedures are required both to enable the institution's selectors to be more ruthless in enforcing its standards and to defend them against the anxieties of doing so.

None of the institutions we studied or visited – with the possible exception of RHB 2 – was content with being just a repository for the damaged and needy. The minimum criteria for admission to these establishments were of course those defined by our pilot study itself: their intake consisted wholly or predominantly of people under 60 with a severe physical handicap. Most institutions, whether professing a horticultural ideology or not, also aspired to be 'homes', and to this end many of them tried to impose a good deal more control over the characteristics of their intake (more than parental homes are able to exercise). They were concerned with the quality of community life and thus with inmates' compatibility with each other. Such institutions might limit their intake, for example, to cripples of high intelligence or from a middle-class background. Several used the trial holiday to corroborate mutual acceptability. Others, like RHB 2, left this to be discovered after admission by the inmates themselves.

Attempts to simplify the selection task usually lead to subsequent problems of rejection. Sheltered workshops, for example, insist on capacity to work as a criterion for admission, but may then be faced with having to discharge those who lose the capacity. (Some workshops accommodate their own retired inmates.) We encountered other institutions in which inmates who become incontinent or need heavy nursing are required to leave. Most try to screen out candidates who are neurotic or show other symptoms of mental instability, and some are adept at disposing of inmates who have developed such symptoms. Only half the institutions we visited explicitly aimed to provide a home for life and to keep their inmates until they died. As in 'real' homes, however, the proviso was made that inmates requiring surgery or becoming otherwise seriously ill would be admitted to hospital; and institutions varied a good deal in their interpretation of such a policy.

In this respect, many institutions were faced with difficulties over their stipulated age-range. A number of them had been specifically set up to provide an alternative for younger people who until that time had no option but to spend the rest of their lives – possibly thirty years or so – in a geriatric ward. In practically every institution, however, we encountered a different age-requirement. One, for example, had been opened to cater especially for the 30-55 age-group because sponsors felt that the needs of this group were overlooked. Another voluntary home had raised the upper limit for admission from 40 to 50. Two units (apart from RHB 2) had virtually no age-limit at all. One of these had inmates ranging from the age of 19 to over 80, though it was trying to encourage a younger clientele. The other intended to go on taking people of all ages; its head drew an analogy with the family, which should be able to accommodate all the seven ages of man.

To prescribe an age-range raises the question of what to do when inmates grow out of it. Of the institutions we visited, only two pursued a rigorous policy of exporting residents to a geriatric unit once they reached the upper limit. Both were RHB units. Four institutions with a specific age-range either had no clearly defined policy as to what happened to people when they reached the top of the range or, having previously decided that they should be exported, found the actual process too painful, not only for inmates but also for staff. One was therefore building an extension to house those above the age-limit, while two others were deferring decisions; the fourth has since capitulated and is now committed to keeping its inmates until death. Some newer institutions that have set an upper age-limit but have not yet had occasion to enforce it may also capitulate when they are actually faced with expelling a long-standing inmate.

Thus, either through having failed to establish in the first instance a realistic policy about an acceptable range of age and incapacity or else through having failed to enforce such a policy, a number of institutions are finding themselves with a population markedly older, more static, and more heavily handicapped than they originally envisaged. An additional factor is that some people with such progressive illnesses as muscular dystrophy have confounded the experts by surviving much longer in a relatively benign institutional setting than had been predicted. The upshot is that a young newcomer to such an institution may find that it does not differ greatly from the type of geriatric unit it was designed to replace.

If we turn back now to the problems of the selectors, we can see a little more clearly the nature of the conflicts to which they are exposed. We can see also that the existence of explicit criteria, even if they are not particularly relevant, may provide some defence for the selectors in their handling of rejection. Note, for example, that the consultant of RHB 1 still clung to the upper age-limit for admission long after he had lowered his standard for mental alertness which, because it was ill defined, was much more difficult to enforce in the face of the pressures on him. But by lowering this standard he was changing the character of the community in a direction that made it much less relevant to insist on the upper age-limit of 45.

We witnessed in a voluntary home an example of the way in which admission criteria are used as a defence against having to face the human problems involved in selection/rejection. The selection subcommittee on this occasion had two tasks to perform: first, to choose candidates from a fairly long waiting-list and either place them on a short list or take them off the waiting-list altogether; and, second, to choose a candidate from the short list to fill a vacancy. We had anticipated that this latter task in particular, which would entail considering the individual circumstances of each applicant in some detail and reaching a decision, would be a painful one for the group. In the event we heard very little of the individual circumstances of the candidates. We learnt that the vacancy to be filled was in a four-bedded room occupied by male residents: this obviously

103

debarred consideration of the female applicants from the short list. Next, we learnt that the bed was one supported by the Regional Hospital Board; this automatically removed from consideration those people on the short list who were supported by local authorities. And since the short list included only one male not supported by a local authority, the decision made itself.

We are not suggesting, of course, that multiple criteria always are or can be used in this way to detoxicate decision-making. When they cannot, the shared responsibility for rejection that the committee procedure provides is a second line of defence. The biases of those who have been personally exposed to the often harrowing needs of candidates can be counteracted by the more detached, institutional view that the remaining members of the committee bring to the discussion.

By contrast, in institutions where the assessment and the decision are made by the same person – the consultants for the RHB units and the respective local welfare officers for the local authority home – the pressures of need are more difficult to resist and standards more difficult to maintain. The whole character of such an institution tends to undergo a change: it becomes increasingly a last resort for those who cannot be accommodated anywhere else. Moreover, it becomes markedly more difficult for the head of the institution – especially where, as in these examples, he is the passive recipient of others' referrals – to exercise any positive internal leadership. The resultant institutional culture is at best non-supportive and at worst repressive.

THE EXPERIENCE OF ADMISSION

Having crossed the boundary into an institution, many inmates display apathy and withdrawal and a few are bitter and angry. There are some, however, who feel liberated and enriched by the move. Differences of personality are obviously relevant, but do not seem to account sufficiently for the variations in attitude. Two factors emerge as crucial: the extent to which the prospective inmate was involved in deciding when and where to be admitted; and his perception of the kind of institution he was entering.

The Role of the Prospective Inmate

Many of the inmates we interviewed had apparently played no part in the transactions that led up to their admission. Often, as the following responses suggest, they seem to have been treated and to have behaved as packages, being posted from one place to another:

'It was arranged. I don't know the details.'
'I forget how it happened.'
'I suppose the LCC got in touch with the RHB and they arranged it.'
'The doctor sent me when my daughter was going away for a holiday.'
'It was chosen for me. The welfare told me there was a vacancy.'
'I think my husband wanted me to come.'

In other instances, although the inmate had been a party to the decision, it was a case of bowing to the inevitable, and no real choice was involved:

Mr Fairbairn, having contracted a progressive disease, was forced to give up his professional career and a few years later entered an institution. He chose this one because it was within visiting distance for his wife. When we saw him he was depressed and bitter both about his own situation and about the particular institution in which he found himself. Having recently written for the inmates' *Newsletter* a short story which reflected very clearly his acute feeling of desolation and loss, he had been severely reprimanded by the matron for introducing depression into what she claimed to be an otherwise 'happy home'. His decision to enter the institution had been precipitated by gastric influenza: his inability to reach the lavatory quickly enough was the last straw. He spoke of the strain he had been imposing on his wife and clearly felt that he had failed her. He believed that he could have remained in his own home longer had it been within

reach of a day centre where he could have been cared for while
his wife was at work. This would have reduced his feeling of
being completely cut off, of being 'a forgotten man . . . wait-
ing for death. . . . . Here you just moulder. When you
become sufficiently incapacitated they stick you in bed – and
the sooner the better.'

Except where the marriage has already collapsed, as in the case
of Mrs Atkins, the move from a marital home to an institution
is especially difficult. It evokes in each spouse feelings both of
having failed and of having been let down. Until these feelings
have been articulated and worked out, no rational decisions are
possible. Indeed, our case-histories confirmed that both married
and single inmates who saw themselves as having made real
choices had first come to terms with the problems of separation:

Miss Green was severely crippled as the result of an accident
in her early teens. When efforts at rehabilitation could
achieve no further improvement she returned to live with
her parents who cared for her for over twenty years. She
realized that as they aged the task of caring for her was
becoming more difficult and that ultimately it would prove
impossible. She had for several years been spending a few
weeks' holiday at the institution where we met her, and she
was able to arrive at the decision to enter that particular
unit while her parents were still capable of looking after her.

Despite the fact that he had suffered from muscular dystrophy
since he was a child, Mr Hathaway had continued to lead an
active life in his home village, going out in all weathers in
his manually operated wheelchair and undertaking a certain
amount of work at home. A domestic crisis led to his entering
hospital: his mother who looked after him needed hospital
treatment. His own stay in hospital was looked upon as a
temporary event, not exceeding a period of three months.
Even for this temporary period, however, Mr Hathaway
managed to exercise some choice, in that he specifically
asked for and obtained admission to an experimental arthritic
unit. Eventually it became clear that Mr Hathaway's mother
was not going to be able to cope with looking after him again

and that he was likely to be in hospital permanently. From the outset, he had been unhappy in the restricted world of the unit. On his first day he was put to bed at 2 o'clock in the afternoon, although he was later allowed to get up for supper. When he questioned being put to bed he was told that the doctor would want to examine him; but the same thing happened the next day. He gave up asking why he was put to bed in the afternoons and he also gave up the fight against going to bed early in the evenings. He passed his time with leather-work, crosswords, letter-writing, and reading. He feels that he was fortunate to move to his present institution after only a year. He learnt of it through a television programme. His thought that he should apply for admission was reinforced by letters from members of his family who had also seen the programme and decided that this institution would be more suitable for him. Now he again leads a relatively active life, makes extensive use of the workshops and other facilities, has mechanical aids to increase his independence, and does not have to go to bed at an unreasonable hour.

Our evidence indicates that individuals who have been personally responsible for the decision to enter an institution have arrived at a more mature acceptance of their disability and its consequences than have those who have taken no part in the process. The latter are likely to deny the reality of the situation in which they need a great deal of care. People with supportive family backgrounds are clearly in a better position to exercise a realistic choice as to their future. And where inmates have also chosen the particular institution they are in, on the basis of the experience of a visit or a holiday there, they are much more likely to become involved in its life and where possible to share responsibility in its affairs. Both they and the institution are more dynamic as a result.

Characteristics of the Institution
There were, however, systematic differences between the institutions: a significantly larger proportion of the inmates in the volun-

tary homes said both that they had exercised choice in coming there and that they believed their choice had been the right one.

In the case of one voluntary establishment, prospective inmates had been especially attracted by the apparent freedom it offered in comparison with the restricted life they had in their parental home or in hospital. One man, describing a preliminary assessment holiday there, recalled:

'It was chaos, but there was something about the community that made me feel I'd like to come.'

He was at that time on the waiting-list of an institution much nearer his own home but he nevertheless applied for admission to this one. This particular institution had received some publicity as 'a pioneer venture' and 'an experiment in social living', which probably attracted the interest of more enterprising people. Several had seen references to it either in articles or on television and had applied as a result.

In the next three chapters we shall be focusing on differences in the internal life of residential institutions. Here we are concerned with differences as they present themselves in the import process itself. There is little doubt that in VH 1 and VH 2, and some other voluntary homes, the more stringent admission criteria themselves had a great deal to do with the more positive attitude of entrants. In fact the two are likely to reinforce each other in a way that makes it difficult to say whether the chicken or the egg comes first. In any type of enterprise there tends to be a correlation between a rigorous selection procedure and the quality of the candidates it attracts. Certainly, the institution that exercises positive control over the admission boundary is the more likely to take responsibility for the inmates it selects, and its acceptance of them as individuals is correspondingly greater. By this means it is also doing something to counteract the social rejection that is the corollary of admission. The selection process itself suggests that the institution offers a distinctive way of dealing with the problems of a 'limbo' sub-society of the disabled; and the quality of the entrants it obtains makes it the more likely that it will achieve this distinctiveness. Or, to put it in another way, the process of selection creates the belief that the institution is something worth joining, as opposed to a repository, and this becomes a self-fulfilling prophecy.

As we have seen, however, institutions that impose firm selection criteria find it hard to maintain them in the face of human need. Ultimately, they are able to maintain their standards only if other institutions are available to take their rejects. And since the less selective institutions undoubtedly face greater difficulties in providing a benign psychosocial environment, the gap between the best and the worst is likely to be perpetuated or widened. However, we would not regard this as inevitable. An institution that establishes admission criteria, such as mental alertness, which it is unable to insist upon in practice, is building failure into the system. If, on the other hand, it redefines its task specifically in terms of catering for those in immediate need, imposes this as a positive criterion for selection, and rigorously rejects all but the most urgent cases, then it stands a greater chance of finding effective ways of performing its task.

CHAPTER 7

The Conversion Process

1: Physical Care

We have cited one or two examples of cripples who have themselves sought admission to an institution in the belief that it would give them opportunities for a richer life than they had at home. But they differ from the overwhelming majority of inmates only in having anticipated a reality that has been the determining factor in the admission of the others: the individual cannot physically cope with his daily living requirements, and insufficient help is available in his household to enable him to stay at home.

The threshold of coping varies between one household and another. A devoted mother or wife, especially if backed by community resources, can go on providing every aspect of physical care for a cripple who is as incapable as an infant of doing anything for himself. At the other extreme, a relatively lightly handicapped person living alone may progressively find that the various tasks of looking after himself, though individually each is quite manageable, have cumulatively reached a point at which he can no longer muster the effort and time that they require.

What all inmates have in common, therefore, is their need for at least some physical help or care; and, correspondingly, what all these institutions have in common is that they exist to provide it. In other words, every institution must incorporate a system of activities through which various resources of physical help are mobilized in order to deal with the physical requirements of the inmates, who are the throughput of the system. Institutions vary, however, in the extent to which this system of physical care dominates the total system or leaves room for other systems of activity that permit inmates to relate to the institution in other ways. We shall discuss this type of variation in the chapters that follow. Here we shall concentrate on another type of variation (not unconnected with it), which has to do with the way in which physical care itself is provided.

Broadly corresponding to the warehousing and horticultural models of residential care that we identified in Chapter 5, we can distinguish between two approaches to the task of physical care. In the former, the inmates are sets of part-objects which have to be processed: bodies which have to be cleaned and dressed, stomachs which have to be filled, bowels which have to be emptied. The resources of the institution are mobilized to carry out these processes as efficiently as possible. In the latter, the inmates are individuals who have available to them various resources through which they are able to deal with their problems of washing, dressing, eating, defecating, and so forth.

These bald descriptions of the two approaches are of course over-simplified and exaggerate the differences that actually exist. No real-life institution wholly conforms to either model and in many the inmate experiences a range of approaches at the hands of different members of staff. There are nevertheless substantial overall differences between one institution and another, especially in the way in which the boundary between the institution and its inmates is defined.

THE DEGREE OF PHYSICAL HELPLESSNESS

Medical definitions of physical incapacity, in terms, for instance, of the amount of movement remaining in arm, hand, or finger, cannot directly be translated into the meaning of the incapacity in the life-space of the individual. Beatrice Wright draws a useful distinction between a disability and a handicap:

'A disability is a condition of impairment having an objective aspect that can usually be described by a physician. . . . A handicap is the cumulative result of the obstacles which disability interposes between the individual and his maximum functional level' (Wright, 1960, p. 9).

But this is not quite enough: the notion of 'maximum functional level' needs to be qualified. To take an obvious example, deafness will be catastrophic for a pianist, as will blindness for a painter; but if the disabilities are reversed their respective handicaps will be less severe. As Selwyn Goldsmith points out:

'A physical attribute is . . . a physical handicap only when it constitutes a barrier to the achievement of specific goals' (Goldsmith, 1967, p. 13).

This more precise definition, however, still does not deal with the problem of comparing one person's handicap with another's: goals tend to be personal and idiosyncratic. Elsewhere, Goldsmith (1966) has partly overcome this problem by identifying certain goals which, by their very ordinariness, are virtually universal. He has suggested a functional classification of handicap, which we have followed here, in terms of five daily living activities: dressing, washing, bathing, feeding, and going to the lavatory.[1] For the able-bodied adult these represent such simple goals that he seldom pauses to think about his ability to achieve them by himself. Almost all inmates of these institutions, on the other hand, need assistance for one or more of these five activities. The extent to which they need it is thus a useful index of their handicap and correspondingly of their dependence.

Tables 12-16 show the number of inmates of the institutions studied who received full assistance, some assistance, or no assistance in each of the five activities. Of the headings used in these tables, 'full assistance' and 'no assistance' are self-explanatory, but 'some assistance' is less precise. In the case of dressing, it may mean that the individual can manage to get his clothes on but is unable to do up his buttons or put on his shoes and socks.

It will be seen that fewer people required help with washing (which refers to limited washing of face and hands in a handbasin) than with any other activity, whereas, as might be expected, most help was required for bathing.

[1] Townsend (1962, pp. 257-84) earlier developed a fuller 'measure of incapacity for self-care' for use with the elderly.

TABLE 12   *Assistance in dressing*

| Institution | Number of inmates receiving: | | | |
	Full assistance	*Some assistance*	*No assistance*	*Total*
VH 1	21	11	7	39
VH 2	15	4	2	21
LA 1	9	18	20	47
RHB 1	14	7	3	24
RHB 2	8	6	2	16
Total	67	46	34	147

TABLE 13   *Assistance in washing*

| Institution | Number of inmates receiving: | | | |
	Full assistance	*Some assistance*	*No assistance*	*Total*
VH 1	7	9	23	39
VH 2	10	1	10	21
LA 1	4	4	39	47
RHB 1	10	3	11	24
RHB 2	8	1	7	16
Total	39	18	90	147

TABLE 14   *Assistance in bathing*

| Institution | Number of inmates receiving: | | | |
	Full assistance	*Some assistance*	*No assistance*	*Total*
VH 1	32	4	3	39
VH 2	19	1	1	21
LA 1	20	21	6	47
RHB 1	19	5	—	24
RHB 2	13	3	—	16
Total	103	34	10	147

TABLE 15   *Assistance in feeding*

Institution	Number of inmates receiving:			
	Full assistance	Some assistance	No assistance	Total
VH 1	19	12	8	39
VH 2	2	5	14	21
LA 1	5	8	34	47
RHB 1	11	5	8	24
RHB 2	6	3	7	16
Total	43	33	71	147

TABLE 16   *Assistance in going to the lavatory*

Institution	Number of inmates receiving:			
	Full assistance	Some assistance	No assistance	Total
VH 1	3	9	27	39
VH 2	15	1	5	21
LA 1	7	8	32	47
RHB 1	13	5	6	24
RHB 2	10	1	5	16
Total	48	24	75	147

Table 17 consolidates these five tables to produce a scale of physical dependence. Inmates are ranked on a scale from 5 to 0 according to the number of activities in which they receive full or some assistance. This shows that RHB 1 has a high concentration of inmates who are dependent for all five activities, and that LA 1 is the only institution in which more than half of the inmates are dependent for two activities or fewer. A similar pattern emerges from *Table 18*, which shows the extent to which inmates were dependent or independent for movement within the building.

The information for these tables was obtained from interviews with inmates. Their estimates of the help they received erred sometimes on the conservative side. Discrepancies between an individual's self-rating and the rating of him by a staff member were most marked when the activity concerned was the use of the lavatory. A few inmates in one institution, for example, said that they required no help whatever, when in fact they had permanent in-dwelling catheters. (It may be noted that of the eighteen inmates of RHB 1 shown in *Table 16* as receiving some or full assistance in going to the lavatory, twelve were said by the staff to be incontinent, some doubly so.) While such discrepancies are partly explicable in terms of a misunderstanding between interviewer and inmate, they point also to some sensitivity over having to admit the need for help with excretory functions. Where possible we checked for such distortion and have corrected for it in the tables.

TABLE 17   *Scale of dependence for daily living activities*

Institution	(Most dependent) 5	4	3	(Least dependent) 2	1	0	Total	Mean
VH 1	8	9	13	4	2	3	39	3·2
VH 2	7	5	4	3	1	1	21	3·5
LA 1	6	2	9	13	11	6	47	2·2
RHB 1	12	3	4	3	2	—	24	3·8
RHB 2	8	1	2	4	1	—	16	3·7
Total	41	20	32	27	17	10	147	3·1

TABLE 18   *Mobility within the building*

Institution	Independent Walks with/without aids	Manually operated wheelchair	Electrically operated wheelchair	Dependent Immobile without assistance	Total
VH 1	4	18	16	1	39
VH 2	3	6	9	3	21
LA 1	17	24	1	5	47
RHB 1	—	11	1	12	24
RHB 2	3	5	3	5	16
Total	27	64	30	26	147

Although we can be satisfied, given these adjustments, that the tables present a reasonably accurate picture of the assistance actually given and received, a further source of distortion still remains and this is much more difficult to correct. To paraphrase Goldsmith's definition, independence is a function not only of the capacities of the individual but also of the relationship between him and his environment in terms of the resources that are available to him and the way in which they are used. A cripple in a wheelchair travelling from one floor to another is helpless if he has stairs to negotiate but independent if there is a lift (provided always that the controls are within his reach).[1]

On the face of it, *Table 17* suggests that the two RHB units have a more severely handicapped population than the other institutions. How far does this higher incidence of dependent behaviour reflect a real difference in intrinsic disability and how far is it the result of an environment that fails to permit or encourage independence? Part of the answer may be revealed in *Table 18*. Although the mean index of dependence in the RHB units is somewhat higher than in the voluntary homes, the proportion of their inmates who are immobile without assistance is six to seven times as high; and in LA 1, where dependence is least, the proportion of immobile inmates is nearly as high as in VH 2 and much higher than in VH 1. Without electrically operated wheelchairs, immobility in VH 1 and VH 2 would be much greater.

THE PROVISION OF PHYSICAL CARE

Residential institutions generally differentiate between caring and other staff. Caring staff, who provide physical services to the inmates, include state registered nurses, state enrolled nurses, and unqualified auxiliaries and orderlies. The remaining staff are engaged in cooking, cleaning, maintenance of buildings and grounds, administration, and so on. Occasionally a cleaner will push a wheelchair in passing; in some institutions even this

---

[1] Selwyn Goldsmith's book, *Designing for the disabled* (1967), is an invaluable source of information on details of this kind that allow buildings to be used by the disabled without being inconvenient for the able-bodied majority of users.

is frowned upon. In general, therefore, inmates are physically dependent on this second category of staff only in an indirect way and may have little or no face-to-face contact with them.

A breakdown of staff numbers and staff–inmate ratios is given in *Table 19*.

TABLE 19   *Staff numbers and staff–inmate ratios*

Institution	No. of inmates	Caring staff	Other staff	Total staff	Caring staff/ inmate ratio	Total staff/ inmate ratio
VH 1	39	$15\frac{1}{2}$	$23\frac{1}{2}$	39	1 : 2·5	1 : 1·0
VH 2	21	8	5	13	1 : 2·6	1 : 1·6
LA 1	47	12	$9\frac{1}{2}$	$21\frac{1}{2}$	1 : 3·9	1 : 2·2
RHB 1	24	$20\frac{1}{2}$	$14\frac{1}{2}$	35	1 : 1·2	1 : 0·7
RHB 2	16	6	—	6	1 : 2·7	1 : 2·7
Total	147	62	$52\frac{1}{2}$	$114\frac{1}{2}$	1 : 2·4	1 : 1·3

Notes: (1) Part-time staff are shown as equivalent full-time staff.
(2) In units VH1 and LA 1, the number of caring staff was increased during our study. The staff ratios in RHB 1 and RHB 2 are misleading in that at the time the figures were collected the staff in RHB 1 also looked after a fluctuating number of patients – up to 17 – in a linked convalescent unit, while RHB 2 had no domestic staff of its own, being serviced by the hospital of which it was a part.

We shall discuss later the breakdown between trained and untrained staff and the controversy over whether or not the skills of trained nurses are needed. The essential point to be noted here is that the activities of physical care, whether carried out by trained or untrained staff and whether over-provided or underprovided, are predominantly concerned with helping inmates in the daily living activities tabulated above. This is clear from the following account by a part-time member of our staff who spent a month as a nursing assistant:

'I was paired up with a qualified staff nurse to attend to four of the more badly handicapped patients who need the most complete physical care and attention – none have the use of their legs, some can use their arms a little, some are able only to move their heads. . . . The physical aspect of the work is hard as these patients have to be lifted in and out

117

of bed, to be turned over – in fact all their moving has to be done for them. We were briefed at 9.30 and working in pairs we had to get up four people and have them washed and dressed for lunch at 12.30. The time spent with each person would vary considerably according to their needs. . . . We had two very disabled people who could only move their heads, and two much less disabled whom we only had to help a little.

We started by changing the draw sheet for Mrs D, one of the very disabled, and giving her a drink through a plastic straw (the most disabled had extra drinks every two hours). We then helped one of the more mobile patients to the lavatory where we left her while we went to wash Mrs T, the other very disabled woman. After a quarter of an hour we went back to Mrs M who can move the upper part of her body quite well. She washed her upper half at the wash-basin, from her wheelchair, then we washed the rest of her on the bed. We next helped her to dress – do her hair, face, etc. – and put her back into her chair. Altogether we lifted her in and out of the chair/bed five times. Next we made the bed and went back to Mrs T. Since Mrs M is fairly active it was quite important to get her up and about comparatively early. I should think we spent about twenty minutes with her.

By 10.15 we were back with Mrs T. It took us longer to finish getting her ready; she had a hoist over her bed which has slings which go under the arms and knees. This helps considerably with the lifting but the hoist has still to be wound up and swung across the bed over the commode chair. She is dressed in the chair as this is easier for both her and the dressers. She also has a bed with an electrically operated top half, so that she can be sat up for meals and drinks, and a special ripple mattress which consists of two parallel sets of plastic tubes in which the air is alternated every few seconds to relieve pressure. Mrs T is up and outside in her chair an hour later. We make her bed and go to help Miss H. She is fairly mobile and has already washed herself – the staff nurse rubbed her back and we help her into her commode chair where she will dress herself. By now it is 11.30

and we leave the beds to go for a quarter-hour coffee break.

At 11.45 we are back with Mrs D who shares a room with Miss H. She was very wet and dirty again – we did the usual washing, rubbing, and moving into a commode chair by hoist – then dressing and doing hair and face; this took the last three-quarters of an hour and another couple of nurses helped us out by making Miss H's bed which we had left unmade. During all these operations we chatted fairly casually to the people with whom we were working with varying degrees of communication. Only Miss H could talk perfectly clearly and she can move more freely than the others as only her lower legs are affected so far. Throughout the day on this wing the ratio of nurses to patients was one to two.'

On the basis of this and other similar accounts and our own observations we would estimate that an individual member of the caring staff spends on average between 50 and 75 per cent of the working day providing services that involve direct physical contact with inmates, the remainder of the time being taken up with ancillary tasks such as bed-making, tidying up, and personal laundry, and with resting and gossiping. Let us say that the direct services take up to six hours out of a nine-hour shift. If the overall ratio of caring staff to inmates is 1 : 2, this means that the individual inmate is receiving physical care for only three hours per day, and many inmates, of course, will be receiving care for substantially shorter periods. Yet the staff member's experience is dominated by the task of providing physical care – and providing it, moreover, to the most heavily handicapped. Obvious though this point is, we believe it is important for its effect on staff members' perceptions of inmates' incapacities. Based on this experience, their generalizations about inmates as a category are likely to be biased.

INTERPERSONAL PROBLEMS OF DEPENDENCY

We turn now to examine the relationship between the provider and the recipient of physical care.

The Problem for Inmates

The degree of physical dependency that obtains in these institutions is met during normal adult life only in special circumstances, such as illness, or in old age. The only other period characterized by such extreme dependence is infancy and early childhood. The emotions, both positive and negative, around in this early period of helplessness are both intense and subject to rapid fluctuation (Klein, 1959). At one moment the child deeply loves and admires his parents; at the next he may experience strong feelings of anger, envy, and resentment at their power over him and at their relationship with each other from which he may feel excluded. Since he is not able to distinguish between the emotions that are inside him and the people or objects that arouse them, or between his impulses and their effects, his negative feelings give rise to guilt and anxiety about the damage that he imagines he has inflicted on the parent-figures. Within a secure parent–child relationship, the child will have ample evidence that his anger has not inflicted permanent damage. He discovers, too, that he is neither omnipotent nor impotent and he learns to assert his independence in some areas and to accept his dependence in others. On the other hand, if the parental relationship is insecure and unhappy, or if the child undergoes long periods of separation from his parents, he may believe that his own negative impulses have proved utterly destructive or that he is being punished for having them. Since many of those whose disability dates from birth or early childhood have spent long periods in hospitals or homes away from their parents, they have had in fantasy, if not in fact, confirmation of such a belief. And they will not have learnt to transform their aggressive feelings into self-reliance and independence. It is therefore to be expected that they should have more difficulty than most of us in coping with their own negative impulses.

Those who have been crippled later in life are not exempt. The experience of unrelieved helplessness not surprisingly tends to reactivate the emotions associated with their earlier infantile dependence. For most adults such lapses into helplessness are temporary and short-lived. Even so, there is evidence that when we take on temporarily dependent roles, such as hospital patient, primitive emotions are readily aroused and are not always controllable. For the cripple, the dependency is far from temporary and, for inmates of the kinds of institution we are discussing, is progressive. Mature ways of dealing with it are correspondingly more difficult to develop.

The important point is, then, that most inmates have retained or reverted to the physical dependence of childhood, and have done so, moreover, in a setting that has ceased to be dependable. As we noted in Chapter 5, many have a history of continual rejections and all share the social rejection that is inherent in admission to institutions of this class. Consciously or unconsciously, they bring with them both the hope that the new institutional environment will prove reliable and the fear of another rejection. Daily situations of infantile dependence tend to mobilize extreme and infantile strategies for dealing with these hopes and fears. Every institution has, in varying numbers and proportions, some inmates who seek to secure the continuing attention they need by excessively placatory and conforming behaviour, and others who strive for attention by a demandingness that seems calculated to test the limits of the staff's patience and tolerance. If the limits are over-reached, then the inmate 'proves' that he is unwanted.

The Problem for Staff

If a residential institution is to fulfil its function of catering for the physically helpless and rejected, it must provide a dependable setting. In theory, at least, it is better placed to do so than the family. It is better able to provide continuity of care: if staff members leave, fall ill, or die, others can be found to take their place. It is also in a position to be more selective about the qualifications of caring staff, whereas competence in looking after children is seldom used as a criterion in selecting candidates for motherhood.

The task demands staff who, in addition to being able to perform the acts of physical care, do not have unresolved problems about their own dependency. A mature person can accept that others are dependent upon him without either resisting this on the one hand or wishing to exert, or being manipulated into exerting, complete control over them on the other.

Many of those who worked in the institutions we studied, as well as those who gave voluntary help, were in this sense mature. A person is often attracted to the work because he or a member of his family has some experience of illness or disability that has led him to feel especially sympathetic towards or interested in the disabled. Others – and this includes nursing, domestic, and administrative staff alike – have felt drawn to the work because they prefer 'a worthwhile job'. Their satisfaction comes from knowing that what they do, even if it is simply cleaning the building rather than caring for individuals, helps the disabled in some way:

'I enjoy the work. You feel you've done something. In other jobs you filled your time in and got paid.'

But institutions set up to deal with dependency are by their very nature liable to attract to staff positions some who have been unable to come to terms with their own dependency in a mature way. Such people may go on searching for situations that allow them to experience a relationship in which they are perpetually dependent or in which they can derive proof of their own superiority from repeated evidence that others are dependent upon them. 'In the land of the blind, the one-eyed man is king.'

Even the mature often find it difficult to adjust to the staff role. Many (probably more than were able to recall it) were initially apprehensive at the thought of working among grossly disabled people:

'To begin with I was doubtful of my own capacity and strength to cope, both physically and emotionally.'

Some feared that they might find the distorted bodies too repulsive; but they recovered more quickly than they expected. As one person wrote:

'Despite apprehension about coping with people who are not attractive physically, when face to face with Mrs V, who can only move her head, who speaks with great difficulty, whose legs have been permanently fixed apart by surgery and have to be tied together when she goes in a wheelchair, the only real thought I had was "How can I best make her comfortable?" '

Several recalled that their first week or so had been distressing. Support from husbands and families helped them to continue with the job and to learn to accept the inevitability of the situation. One recorded that

'the mutual acceptance of the situation by nurse and patient was infectious. After a month I found it difficult to remember my own apprehensions.'

In retrospect many staff members felt that they had been too sympathetic in their early contacts and had tended to be over-solicitous. They found themselves unable to sustain this attitude indefinitely and also began to realize that it encouraged the inmates to be even more dependent than was necessary.

Evidence from our interviews and observations suggests that those staff who did not acknowledge any problems of adjusting to the work were the ones who also showed themselves to be less than adequate in their relationships with inmates. Mature staff, having faced and overcome the initial problems of adjustment, appeared more able to accept, rather than to deny, the depression associated with severe handicap and to understand intuitively the difficulties of extreme dependency. They found ways of providing intimate physical services without either destroying the inmate's individuality and adult status or surrendering their own and becoming robots. They were better able to interpret and accept the difficult and provocative behaviour of an inmate as an expression of frustration at his impotence rather than as an attack on themselves personally or on the institution. A relationship with such a staff member can help the inmate to discover a mature way of coming to terms with his dependence while retaining an adult identity.

Our findings suggest, however, that this outcome is exceptional, almost accidental. This seems to be because there is no socially sanctioned and culturally supported model for a relationship in which one adult is permanently dependent on another. The nearest available model is the mother–child relationship, but this is obviously far from appropriate. The child is progressively becoming more independent, the crippled inmate progressively less so. The mother is compensated for her increasing dispensability by sharing vicariously in the growth and maturation of the child; the staff member in the institution cannot be sustained by any realistic hopes about the future development of her charges. To respond to the emotional needs of the inmate, the staff member must experience an emotional involvement in the relationship; yet the greater the involvement the greater the stress.

Thus over and above providing the resources through which the physical needs of the inmates are satisfied, the institution provides a means through which this stress is dealt with. The specific relationship between staff member and inmate is modulated by the overall relationship between the institution and its inmates, which encourages certain kinds of behaviour and discourages others.

THE INSTITUTION AND ITS INMATES: TWO MODELS OF PHYSICAL CARE

Institutional Defences against Anxiety

The notion that social structures not only provide means through which a manifest task is performed but also equip members with defences against anxiety is now well established (Bion, 1961; Jaques, 1955; Menzies, 1960). Isabel Menzies in particular has demonstrated how the social structure of a hospital is used by nurses as a defence against the anxieties of their job that arise from the problems of providing intimate physical care and from their encounters with death. She has also shown how the structure is correspondingly distorted into a less effective instrument of task performance, with the result that stress is increased (Menzies, 1960). But at least in a hospital the majority of patients stay for a relatively short time, get better, and go away. While the succession of brief relationships may pose additional problems for the hospital nurse, these are perhaps counterbalanced by the possibility of perceiving the frequency of discharges as satisfying evidence of success.

In residential institutions, in which inmates do not get better, the stress for staff is more acute. Correspondingly, defences such as the depersonalization of the patient, however much one may deplore them in the hospital setting, are for the typical hospital patient a short-lived experience from which he will recover when he returns to his normal social roles outside; whereas in the residential institution that adopts such defences the inmate may have to take on permanently the depersonalized role that is demanded of him. This is a process that has been analysed closely by Erving Goffman in *Asylums* (Goffman, 1961).

We shall try to show here that the warehousing model of residential care tends to reproduce and magnify the problems of the conventional hospital setting. The horticultural model provides an environment within which it is more likely that a mature and effective staff–inmate relationship can develop; but it also, as it must, provides staff with defences, which are sometimes dysfunctional.

We would emphasize the phrase 'as it must'. We see both the stress and the need for defences against it as real and inevitable. Some of the things we saw appalled us and although we have struggled to understand how they have come about, it is difficult to write about them without exasperation. But defensive structures are not the preserve of the 'worst' institutions: they are observable in the 'best' too. Our purpose in discussing them is not to criticize or detract from what is being done but to stimulate the analysis and understanding of what actually happens.

Perhaps this will be clearer if we take a simple example. Fairness and impartiality are unexceptionable values which are universally professed in these institutions and substantially enforced. If a particular inmate appears to be receiving more than his fair share of attention from a staff member, other staff and inmates alike will either overtly protest or at least bring pressure to bear on the individuals concerned. In some institutions extreme measures are taken to achieve fairness. In one, for example, we were told that any gifts of fruit or sweets were scrupulously divided into equal shares. If an outing was arranged, all had to be given an opportunity of going to the same place, even if this meant, because of transport difficulties, that they went in several batches on different days. But even in its less extreme manifestations, this insistence on equality of treatment can be seen as a way of avoiding or denying the reality that different individuals have markedly different needs, emotional as well as physical, and thus require unequal attention. Similarly, in most institutions a duty roster ensures that staff are rotated between the inmates. It can be argued that this is plainly to the benefit of both parties. Some inmates are much more difficult to handle, physically or psychologically, and it would not be fair for the same staff to have to cope with this burden all the time. Equally, some staff are more skilful, or benevolent, than others and it would be hardly fair on an inmate if he were always paired with the least able attendant. These arrangements, however, also have a defensive connotation. By denying that some inmates may prefer less skilled attention from staff they like to more efficient attention from those they dislike, the convention of fairness preserves the interpersonal distance between staff member and inmate as individuals. Avoidance of favouritism can thus inhibit development of a potentially supportive relationship between them.

Another defence mechanism observable in varying degrees in all the institutions studied was the process of scapegoating and/or canonization. Paradoxically, although it runs counter to the values of fairness and impartiality, it coexists with them. It also has a similar function. Insistence that all are equal avoids the difficulties of discriminating between individuals, but it demands the adoption of stereotypes: one applies a label to an individual and relates to the label rather than to the person. Stereotyping leads naturally to scapegoating. If, for instance, as often happens, an inmate is labelled as a trouble-maker and staff proceed to behave towards him as if he were a trouble-maker (while also, one surmises, fellow-inmates project into him the trouble-making bits of themselves), he may find it extremely difficult to escape from the role in which he has been cast.

Although to some extent, therefore, the common problems of providing physical care in all institutions for the incurable, dependent, and rejected lead to common defence mechanisms, we have also observed marked differences between one institution and another. Here we ourselves are of course guilty of stereotyping when we refer to the warehousing and horticultural models. These labels do, however, appear to reflect differences that are systematic. By this we mean that each model represents a coherent set of attitudes and behaviour in terms of a concept of the inmate as a person, a definition of his physical and other needs, and the way in which these are, or are not, provided for.

Concepts of the Inmate as a Person
Staff in warehousing institutions characteristically over-emphasized the amount of physical care required. That is, they exaggerated the numbers requiring special care and seemed unable to differentiate, in talking of inmates generally, between those needing a great deal of care and those needing less. For example, people with multiple sclerosis suffer from tremors and a general difficulty in coordinating limb movements, and often from impairment of speech. In later stages of the disease, they may have uncontrollable fits of laughing or crying and show signs of mental derangement. The tendency in warehousing institutions was to speak of all inmates as though they were on a par with the most advanced cases of multiple sclerosis:

'Most of them are no longer *compos mentis*.'
'They're all doolally, you know.'

Because it is with the most advanced cases that caring staff spend most of their time, such a stereotype, once established, receives perpetual reinforcement. Since inmates in these institutions were perceived as less than whole persons, care and attention were lavished instead on their bodily parts.

By contrast, in institutions that exhibited the horticultural ideology the inmate was regarded as something greater than a collection of more or less defective parts. The possibility was acknowledged that he might have real and legitimate feelings

127

which should be taken into account. Staff were less likely to assume that a speech impairment or a pronounced facial tic was a sign of a deranged mind. For example, when a matron talked to us about Miss Jones, who was in an advanced stage of Friedreich's ataxia, she did not dismiss her as 'doolally', but said how frustrating she must find it not to be able to speak. She did not say, as an attendant in another institution did, 'We have to do their thinking for them'. Instead, she described how, in getting Miss Jones a bedtime drink, it was useless to ask 'What will you have?', because inability to formulate an answer would raise her frustration to an intolerable level; it was better to name the various drinks available, which enabled Miss Jones to indicate the one she preferred.

This difference in attitude was exemplified in the approach to pressure sores. Exponents of the warehousing ideology laid emphasis on the level of skill required to prevent sores from developing or to disperse them once they had formed. On the other hand, an exponent of the horticultural ideology was more likely to look upon sores not as localized physical entities but as psychosomatic phenomena. Describing an inmate who had spent several weeks in hospital after an operation and sustained a large sore as a result, one such staff member said:

> 'It's much more important how you treat the person than how you treat the pressure sore. You have to treat the whole person and not just the sore. Once a person knows they are really cared for the sore is much more likely to heal up.'

Our concern here is not to enter into controversy over the aetiology of pressure sores and right and wrong ways of preventing and treating them (though those in the care of this staff member seemed to have an unusually low incidence), but rather to use the two different approaches to the problem as illustrations of the two different ideologies. Integral to the horticultural model is a concept of the person that relates the part to the whole and the whole to the environment.

More generally, the institutions operating the two models differed over the qualifications required of caring staff and in the use by inmates of mechanical and other aids.

Qualifications for Caring Staff

Staff qualifications are a topic that is frequently debated. Ultimately it is incapable of resolution as an independent issue, in that while the needs of the inmates plainly determine the number and qualifications of staff, the nature and composition of the staff reciprocally determine the type and amount of care given and thus tend to modify the needs of the inmates, both felt and expressed. In discussing this debate we must avoid exaggerating the differences between the institutions. On the one hand, almost all the staff we interviewed, in whatever type of institution, differentiated the task of their institution from that of the conventional hospital. Most said that they were trying to provide a 'home'. (One exception was the matron of an RHB unit who saw its task as having a strongly medical orientation approximating to that of a neurosurgical unit.) On the other hand, there was also general agreement that a certain number of trained nursing staff was essential – for example, to spot potential emergencies that might go unnoticed by a lay person and to administer drugs and injections. By and large, too, although one or two of our respondents perceived staff essentially in terms of strong backs and pairs of hands, most gave at least lip-service to the notion that personal qualities were also important. The head of one RHB unit, for instance, said that he wanted sympathy above all in his nurses.

The main point at issue is the proportion of qualified nursing staff. The actual proportions in the institutions studied are given in *Table 20* (which may be compared with *Table 19*).

One argument of those who advocated a higher proportion was that trained staff were particularly necessary for heavy-nursing cases. Now it is clear that where progressive cases are predominant there is a greater need for trained staff; but we noticed that the phrase 'heavy-nursing case' could be given different meanings. Even in speaking about persons whose physical condition seemed to us to be comparable, staff in a warehousing institution said or implied that 'heavy nursing' meant skilled and intensive care, using specialized techniques, whereas in a horticultural setting it meant care that demanded a good deal of lifting and carrying.

TABLE 20   *Breakdown of caring staff by qualifications*

Insti-tution	No. of inmates	State registered nurses	State enrolled nurses	Others	Total	Caring staff/ inmate ratio	Trained nursing staff/ inmate ratio
VH 1	39	4	$2\frac{1}{2}$	9	$15\frac{1}{2}$	1 : 2·5	1 : 6·0
VH 2	21	2	—	6	8	1 : 2·6	1 : 10·5
LA 1	47	$2\frac{1}{2}$	2	$7\frac{1}{2}$	12	1 : 3·9	1 : 10·4
RHB 1	24	$6\frac{1}{2}$	$3\frac{1}{2}$	$10\frac{1}{2}$	$20\frac{1}{2}$	1 : 1·2	1 : 2·4
RHB 2	16	1	1	4	6	1 : 2·7	1 : 8·0
Total	147	16	9	37	62	1 : 2·4	1 : 5·9

A second argument for trained staff was that qualified nurses were generally more efficient, even if the content of the job did not require specialized nursing skills. And, of course, a great deal of the physical care given in ordinary hospitals, as in these institutions, consists of little more than washing, bathing, toileting, changing clothes, bed-making, and feeding. In the words of one attendant, herself untrained:

'Fully trained nurses can probably be very tiresome with routine, but I do think their training has imbued them with a better sense of the importance of thorough physical attention than untrained orderlies. . . . It is not just a question of superior intelligence, as many of the orderlies are university students.'

About 'the importance of thorough physical attention' *per se* there can be no argument. But in institutions operating the horticultural model greater emphasis is given to non-physical aspects of attention. Moreover, it is felt that being 'tiresome with routine' is almost inescapable when trained nurses dominate the staff: they expound a concept of efficiency that runs counter to the values of what is meant by a 'home'. Adaptiveness, flexibility, and an awareness of the needs of the individual are more important.

Thus a high proportion of qualified nursing staff tends to be correlated with the adoption of a warehousing model and is not necessarily correlated with a high degree of physical in-capacity. The latter is more accurately reflected in the overall ratio of caring staff (regardless of qualifications) to inmates. This shows up vividly in a comparison of VH 2 and RHB 1. Both have similarly high proportions – about 60 per cent – of highly dependent inmates (those with ratings of 4 or 5 on the scale of dependence in *Table 17*); but whereas RHB 1 has the highest ratio of nursing staff to inmates (1 : 2·4) VH 2 has the lowest (1 : 10·5). When all caring staff are included the ratios are less discrepant, though RHB 1's ratio of 1 : 1·2 is still the highest. (It remains the highest even after full allowance is made for attendance on convalescent patients; see *Table 19*, note 2.)

The Use of Equipment

The stronger the advocacy of trained staff as the human re-sources of the physical caring process, the less is the use of equipment in this process and the more negative are the atti-tudes of staff towards equipment. Indeed, we postulate that staff attitudes towards the use of electrically operated wheel-chairs are perhaps the best single indicator of the prevailing value system.

In the horticultural model the inmate is encouraged to interact with his environment as much as and for as long as he can. He should not subside into unnecessary helplessness. To this extent anything that enables the individual to maintain his independence is valued. In this respect the effect of the electric wheelchair is striking. In one institution a third of the inmates acquired these chairs as soon as they became available through the National Health Service. This meant that those who would have had to depend on staff to move them were now largely or completely mobile throughout the building (see *Table 18*).

In other institutions those who can no longer propel their own wheelchairs or walk without support may find themselves sitting in one place for hours at a time, dependent on catching the attention of a passing orderly if they want to move, or even to face in a different direction – which can be important for one whose impairment makes reading or a manual occupation such as knitting difficult or impossible. Speech impediments, especially if, as is often the case, the orderly is a foreign worker with only a rudimentary knowledge of English, can make the inmate's efforts to obtain such help frustrating or abortive. Yet inmates in these other institutions were either not encouraged to apply for electrically operated chairs or actively discouraged from applying for them. The head of one of the units we visited insisted that sufferers from neuromuscular disorders could never control them. In his opinion they were suitable only for those who retained full use of hands and arms – and who thereby were presumably capable of operating an ordinary wheelchair. Others resisted on the grounds that the vehicles were dangerous: the inmates would damage walls and furniture and injure the staff. One consultant described them as 'expensive toys'.

It was notable that where a few individuals were equipped with electric wheelchairs in predominantly warehousing settings, they were frequently expected to act as exhibits and to go through a performance to display their virtuosity to visitors. By demanding this performance, staff were effectively underlining the distinctions between the inmates on the one hand and themselves and the visitor on the other, as if they were reluctant to acknowledge that the inmate's diminished helplessness in fact increased the common ground between them.

Unwillingness to contemplate chairs that could increase their users' independence was accompanied by a dearth of aids generally. Standard aids were frequently said to be unsuited to an individual's particular impairments and modification was seldom envisaged. In horticultural environments, on the other hand, considerable ingenuity was exercised by inmates, staff, and outside helpers to overcome an individual's specific problems. The disability (in Beatrice Wright's terms) might be equivalent, but the handicap was reduced. In one institution, a band of helpers came in weekly to work on gadgets for the inmates. (The word 'gadget' here had a positive connotation instead of being used in a pejorative sense.) In another, the resident carpenter devised individual aids – for example, to enable inmates to switch their radios on and off.

132

Financial considerations obviously cannot be ignored. Electronic aids like the Possum, which can convert a flicker of movement in a finger, or even a breath, into energy that will perform a whole range of operations for a quadriplegic, are undoubtedly expensive. And in terms of the values of the wider society, the electric wheelchair, the electric hoist, the pedal-operated WC flushing system, and a host of similar aids can perhaps be dismissed as 'expensive toys', except perhaps to the very limited extent that they can increase the productivity of caring staff. But even if these are ruled out by expense, other resources – ingenuity, creativeness, and willingness to work and pool ideas with the disabled in order to try to solve a problem – are cheaper and no less important, not only in producing the gadgets themselves but in expressing a particular concept of what the caring process is about. (We recall the joy with which a polio victim showed us the hinged back to his wheelchair which enabled him, 'after all these years', to go to the lavatory by himself.) One suspects that staff who reject aids, whether on the ground of expense or on the ground that their inmates are too helpless to manage them, are really expressing an inability to tolerate a measure of independence in those they look after.

The Boundary between the Institution and the Inmate

Essentially, the warehousing model, with its stress on qualified nursing staff, and the horticultural model, with its greater use of non-human aids and gadgets, draw the boundary between the inmates and the institution in different places.

The horticultural ideology asserts the right, and indeed the obligation, of the individual to control the boundary between himself and his environment. The function of caring staff is to help him to help himself and to step into the breach when he cannot manage.

In the warehousing model, by contrast, staff take over control of the individual's boundary and remove his areas of discretion. This is the logical consequence of seeing the inmate as essentially an aggregate of more or less defective parts, rather than as a person. The sentiment quoted earlier – 'We have to do their thinking for them' – sums up this philosophy. This control may be manifested in limitations on freedom of movement within the building even for those who can propel themselves. Sleeping quarters are not uncommonly out of bounds. In one unit, the garden was not explicitly forbidden territory, but a steep step from french windows was not negotiable by wheelchairs and an old ramp, that had once enabled access, was in a state of disrepair and remained so throughout the year during which we paid periodic visits. Control in this institution was also extended to the physiological functions of eating, drinking, and excretion. Eating between meals was forbidden and the liquid intake of incontinent inmates was rationed. In one instance, an attendant preparing nightcaps pointed out that she was not providing drinks for everyone:

> 'I don't give Mrs Kaye a drink. I tell her she'll only wet the bed. It's not good for them to lie in their own urine.'

Mrs Kaye's feelings in the matter were manifestly irrelevant. The advent of visitors bringing fruit and chocolate upset the routine and staff complained – a complaint that we heard nowhere else – that the main visiting days were followed by a high incidence of vomiting by the inmates. As a corollary of these controls over the intake of food and drink, an unusually high proportion of these inmates were dependent on suppositories, which enabled staff to regulate the frequency and timing of excretion. Suppositories were normally applied only once a week. Although measures such as this invade and erode the physical and psychological boundaries of the individual, both literally and metaphorically, staff not unnaturally did not look upon them in this way. Either they took this régime for granted, accepting it as 'matron's orders', or, if they thought about it at all, they rationalized what they were doing as appropriate to the needs of the inmates or even (as in the case of keeping Mrs Kaye dry) in the inmates' best interests.

Defence Mechanisms and the Reality

We return now to the use of these two models as defence mechanisms. Plainly the warehousing model helps staff to deal with the problems of the dependent relationships by dehumanizing the inmate or at least by taking away his adult status. The inmate is identified with his crippled physique and his drives and needs as an adult human being are parenthetical. He is asked in effect to relinquish these latter aspects of himself and surrender them to the institution. We noticed that staff in warehousing institutions displayed greatest affection towards their most incapacitated inmates – 'the cabbages', as they are sometimes called. By extending the inherent physical dependence of the inmate to dependence in other areas of his life, this model establishes an unequivocal relationship of superiority and inferiority between the giver and the receiver of physical care.

The horticultural or anti-medical model, on the other hand, encourages and helps staff to accept the greater uncertainties of a relationship in which the concept of the adult human being has primacy, and the physical disability is a constraint. The inmate is expected to be as independent as his disability will permit.

Although this second model is manifestly healthier and more positive, both models in fact imply, and impose on inmates, a set of norms which do not wholly reflect the reality of their situation. Thus the inmate must either distort his reality and conform to the norms set for him or be classified as a deviant or failure. While the warehousing ideology can lead to the more obvious faults of depersonalization and even to staff behaviour that is alleged to be sadistic,[1] the horticultural outlook can lead to less obvious distortions. Independence can be over-valued, an end rather than a means. If one asks whether there is any great virtue in an inmate dressing himself unaided in the mornings and getting himself undressed and into bed at night if these activities take up two hours or more a day and he has little

[1] Inmates in one institution told us about the suicide of a fellow-victim. She suffered from multiple sclerosis and was acutely depressed, and one of her few consolations was smoking. The matron, who disapproved, instructed the attendant who took her to the lavatory to leave her there for two or three hours as a means of keeping her away from cigarettes. A day or two later the girl managed to cut her wrists with a razor blade when she was left in a bath. Whatever the truth of this story, it vividly expresses some of the underlying feelings of inmates in a warehousing institution.

strength left over to do anything else, the response is likely to be that if this is what the person wants to do he should be allowed to do it. But this attitude ignores the cultural pressures which may make the individual feel that to seek help is evidence of personal failure. In this way horticultural values (which are more likely than warehousing values to be endorsed by the inmates as well as by the staff) can lead to dogged insistence on independent behaviour, to denial of disability, and to the setting of goals of performance that it is beyond the individual's capacity to attain. Dependency, even when it is appropriate, may become unacceptable. One woman, who in public rumbustiously asserted her independence and claimed that the necessary physical care should be competent but impersonal and unobtrusive, finally confided in private her underlying need for a strong parent-figure on whom she could depend.

Thus insistence on treating inmates as normal adults can be almost as misleading as the more patronizing warehousing attitude. Both ideologies are to that extent means of defending staff from relating to inmates as they really are, without either over- or under-estimating the differences between them and able-bodied 'normals'. And, correspondingly, the ideologies are a defence for the inmates themselves.

CHAPTER 8

The Conversion Process
2: Inmates' Activities

DEPENDENCE AND INDEPENDENCE

By and large, as we have seen, the disabled enter residential institutions because they need a degree of physical care that is not available to them elsewhere. Inevitably, this common need of inmates has an overwhelming effect on the way in which the institution defines its primary task and the role of inmates within it. Caring staff must be available to help them with daily living activities. But even the most physically helpless cripple is more than the passive recipient of physical care. Every inmate has an inner life that goes beyond the dependent relationship and has an individuality expressed in thoughts and feelings and, so far as his capacity will allow, in words and actions. To some extent it is expressed in the context of the physical caring relationship itself, which is thereby made more complex. It also requires independent expression. In this chapter, therefore, we examine what happens to inmates once their day-to-day physical needs have been met – what other roles, if any, are open to them besides that of physical dependency.

The Conflict

Tension and conflict between independence and dependence, between striking out on one's own and returning to the mother's bosom, are central to the process of maturation from infancy onwards. Each person develops his own characteristic way of reconciling these two opposing pulls. The outcome, however, is not a static equilibrium. To be alive and remain sane, the adult must continually be oscillating between the dependent and independent aspects of himself, expressing each in turn. To remain wholly in one posture or the other is in effect to cease to be human. Dependence and independence in this sense have both physical and psychological components. Thus the able-bodied adult in the barber's chair may experience gratification at the attention he is receiving, tinged perhaps with some worry about what may be done to him while he is immobilized; similarly, in acts of independent self-expression the satisfaction he derives may, when he compares his achievements with his aspirations, be tempered by feelings of incompetence or at least of having done less well than he had hoped.

Arguing from this, we postulate that any residential institution set up to cater for people (as opposed to catering merely for maimed bodies) has to provide for their psycho-physical needs for independence as well as for dependence. Organizationally, it is not enough that it creates a system of activities through which to provide physical care, however ably it deals with the concomitant psychological problems of physical dependency; it must also create a parallel system of activities through which inmates find means of expressing their independence. And if we are right in conceiving of the life of a mature adult in terms of a constant process of expressing and reconciling these conflicting aspects of himself, then it follows that in the institution too the inmate should experience some corresponding conflict between his roles in these two systems of activity.

We should perhaps underline here that the distinction we are drawing is not between physical and psychological needs. Initially, we found ourselves looking at the problem in these terms, and at first sight it seems rational to do so. It becomes easy to generalize and say that this 'bad' institution caters only for physical needs, while that 'good' institution caters for psychological needs as well. Such a dichotomy between the physical and the psychological is, however, misleading. Verbal distinctions between body and mind, body and soul, which spring so glibly to the tongue, are admirable illustrations of the thesis that man thinks in terms of polarities and has developed a language that expresses this mode of thinking; but the reality is that the physical and the psychological are indivisible. We hope we have made this clear in the previous chapter by discussing physical care as a psycho-physical process concerned with catering for psycho-physical dependency. Correspondingly, in this chapter we are focusing on provision for psycho-physical self-expression and independence. Although we can still be accused of polarizing, we believe that the dependence–independence dichotomy is a good deal more realistic and meaningful in the experience of living than is the physical–psychological.

In all institutions set up to deal with dependent needs there is a danger that inmates will be perceived only as dependent bodies requiring care and attention. In some institutions this perception is dominant. Inmates are reduced to the lowest common denominator of physical incapacity. Other kinds of needs and drives tend to be discounted. If they are acknowledged at all, they are seen as secondary and subsidiary. Inmates are thought of as more sick, more helpless, or more mentally afflicted by their disease than they really are, apparently in order to justify the philosophy that physical care is all that is necessary. And as Goffman (1961) has shown, such beliefs tend to have the character of self-fulfilling prophecies. Having been lopped to fit the Procrustean bed of the institution, inmates' beliefs about themselves are modified by the staff philosophy and they become in fact diminished.

In reaction against this pattern of pathological dependence, there is now in other institutions an awareness that the individual inmate is more than the sum total of his physical needs, and that meeting these is a means to an end, not an end in itself. But the reaction can lead to another distortion of reality. Inmates may place undue emphasis on achievement and push away the facts of physical dependency. Staff whose *raison d'être* is physical care find that the legitimacy of their role has been removed; their consequent uncertainty is one of the problems we tried to work through at Le Court (cf. Chapter 2). Underlying the philosophy of achievement is the fantasy that by this means the disabled will prove that they are as 'normal' as the able-bodied: their physical disability is merely incidental. This creates the other kind of Procrustean bed which they can seldom be stretched to fit. Failure to recognize the fantasy element can only postpone and make more painful the eventual recognition that the activities and achievements are no substitute for a healthy body; they do not save the victim of a progressive disease from premature decline and death. The denial of depression and despair inherent in this fantasy can lead to destructive conflict within the individual and within the institution as a whole. In Le Court, for example, we became aware of residents' needs to find objects and causes to fight for or against. As we have already said, some conflict is inevitable and fighting may be a sign of health and aliveness; but it can also be a symptom of unresolved internal conflicts which individuals are projecting onto their environment. This is destructive not only because of its effects on others, but more particularly because by means of projection the individuals concerned avoid facing, and therefore resolving, their own internal conflicts.

An ideal institution, perhaps, would make room for both dependency and achievement. The one would not be used to keep the other at bay. Each individual would have the opportunity, the responsibility, and the necessary help to face his own internal conflicts. His capacities would be neither overrated nor underrated. We have certainly observed that inmates who accept the reality of their disabilities are much more likely to find constructive and rewarding ways of using their capacities. One inmate summed this up in what she called 'the three "A"s: Accept, Adjust, Achieve'.

Individual differences have to be recognized. People with multiple sclerosis are not all cabbages; those with polio are not all potential President Roosevelts. While some physically helpless inmates have active brains and a great deal of determination, others, though equally intelligent, are apathetic, and others again with a history of continual rejection or deprivation have great difficulty in forming and maintaining relationships. There are also real differences between institutions in the characteristics of their inmates: in one that caters almost exclusively for very helpless or terminal cases, physical care will be a far more dominant constraint than in another that does not accept people with progressive diseases.

Our observations suggest, however, that the kinds and scope

of inmates' activities in an institution are related less to the individual's specific capacities, or to the average degree of physical care required, than to the prevailing ideology, which supports either dependency or achievement, but seldom both. The attitudes of staff, and of the head of the institution in particular, are of critical significance. In their activities, inmates are affected by, and to some extent collude with, these attitudes.

The Collusive Denial

We would not underestimate the collusiveness of the process. Although we see the perpetual tension between the independent and dependent aspects of the self as intrinsic to maturity, it also has its discomforts and anxieties, which the individual seeks ways of alleviating. Probably all human institutions provide their members with defences against anxiety, and the residential institution is no exception. It provides defences for its inmates as well as for its staff by adopting its own characteristic method of dealing with the two 'conversion processes' we have identified – catering for dependence and independence respectively – and with the conflict or potential conflict between them. We identified two such methods in the institutions we studied.

In a warehousing institution, the emphasis on physical care may be carried to such extremes that there is opportunity for only the most circumscribed activity of any kind. With very few exceptions, inmates are continually forced into a dependent role in all facets of their lives. This results in a withdrawal of interest from the world around them. The body is cared for but any manifestation of individuality is treated as trouble-making and disciplinary measures are introduced to deal with the offender.

In a horticultural institution, where the emphasis is on achievement, the two aspects of the conversion process seem characteristically to be split between staff and inmates, a formal staff organization being responsible for care and, in conflict with it, an informal inmate organization for activities.

In the sections that follow, we shall examine the effects of these patterns first on social relationships and recreational activities, then on work and work-substitutes, and finally on the involvement of inmates in the running of the institution.

SOCIAL AND RECREATIONAL ACTIVITIES

Choices within the Institution

Self-expression and maintenance of individual identity are
closely linked to the exercise of choice; to do this or to do that,
to relate to one person rather than another, to be with others
or to remain alone, to go out or to stay in, and so on. Institutional living constricts opportunities for making such choices:
for the most part, the inmate has to eat, sleep, work, and play
all with the same people and within the confines of the same
building. Consequently, if individuality is to be preserved,
special efforts are required to counteract the impoverishment
of the institutional environment.

Examples from two cases will contrast the opportunities that
institutions provide for inmates to pursue their own interests:

> Mr Long was writing a book. For the extensive private study
> and research involved, he needed solitude; but he shared his
> room with others. He therefore used to read and write in
> the chapel, where he could be assured of peace. No one
> objected.

In this institution, inmates were free to follow their own interests
and all the facilities of the building were open to everybody
without question.

> Mr Mitchell, a music-lover, brought his record-player with
> him when he was admitted. However, he was not allowed
> to use it on the ground that there was no room available:
> wards were out of bounds in the daytime (and used for sleep-
> ing in the evening), the public lounge was reserved for
> television, the workshop was open only when a member of
> staff was in charge, and one remaining large room, which was
> in use only two days a week, was at other times kept locked.
> Mr Mitchell's friends wanted to take him out to concerts but
> permission was refused. He did not submit readily and it was
> generally agreed that he was a difficult man to get on with.
> The matron decided that he was 'a disturbing influence' and
> arranged for him to be sent to a psychiatric hospital. In due
> course he returned, a subdued character who made no further

demands. Indeed, when we saw him it was difficult to believe the stories we heard of his previous turbulence. He seemed totally compliant. Like so many of his fellow-inmates he divided his time between basketry (nodding off to sleep over his task) and simply sitting, virtually out of contact with those around him.

The early part of Mr Mitchell's case-history is based on hearsay evidence from other inmates and staff and is therefore not necessarily reliable. But about the limits that staff placed on inmates' movements in this institution there is no doubt. Where parts of the building are put out of bounds and inmates are not, for example, allowed to use the garden or even to sit in the hall to watch people coming and going, it is small wonder that they become withdrawn and apathetic and appear to staff and visitors alike as having very few interests. One might then conclude that their limited environment is appropriate to their limited aspirations and that they would be unable to make use of richer opportunities. And this conclusion would probably be correct. To the extent that the institution makes choices on behalf of the inmate, his individuality is diminished, and the consequent deteriorating cycle is difficult or even impossible to arrest.

An important factor in this respect is the extent to which the institution controls the transactions of inmates with the outside world. We shall examine first the receipt of visitors and then the excursions that inmates make into the environment.

The Institutional Boundary: the Receipt of Visitors

The warehousing institution guards its charges jealously and erects substantial barriers between them and the community outside. When visiting hours are confined to afternoons or very early evenings, even relatives who live within easy reach of an institution can, if they have regular jobs, visit only at weekends. Staff often appeared unaware of the effect on inmates of imposing strict visiting hours. For example, one nursing assistant who asserted:

'This is the residents' home and not a hospital'

seemed not to notice any inconsistency when she added:

'They used to have visitors here until 11 o'clock at night. Well, you couldn't have that. They have to leave at 8 o'clock now.'

Many institutions, however, operate an open-door policy whereby visitors are free to call at almost any time. Only exceptionally, of course, are relatives able – or indeed willing – to visit daily, but our observations suggest that this policy generates more visits. Thus the attenuation of relationships with friends and kin, which is a corollary of admission to residential care, is somewhat reduced.

Also important in maintaining the quality of his relationships with people outside is the extent to which the inmate can take the role of host. Regulation of visiting hours implies that it is the institution, rather than the individual inmate, that is being visited, and the role of host is correspondingly taken over by staff. Freedom to receive visitors and to entertain them in his own room helps the inmate to maintain his individuality and not to become so submerged into an undifferentiated institutional group. If he is able to offer a visitor a meal occasionally (paid for out of his pocket money) or simpler hospitality in the form of a cup of tea and a biscuit, he can experience, however temporarily, a giving rather than a taking role. We have sometimes heard staff speak with disapproval of those inmates (usually women) who spent a great deal of their pocket money on presents for their children or other members of the family. To staff this seemed a waste and we were told it was often far more than the inmate could afford. Yet this might be the only way in which a mother could show her continuing affection for her children, and to her it was clearly a symbol of more active forms of care that she wished she could still give them.

Apart from pre-existing friends and relatives, most of the other outsiders who cross the boundary into the institution are voluntary helpers. Again, institutions vary in the way in which they regulate relationships between helpers and individual inmates. Some institutions limit both the number of helpers and the tasks they may do. The head of one RHB unit, for example, saw fund-raising as the most appropriate activity;

and about the uses to which the money was put inmates were not consulted. If outside helpers came into contact with inmates at all, it was in an impersonal role: for instance, a weekly round with a mobile shop or library. They were discouraged from taking an interest in inmates as people and developing relationships with them. By contrast, we encountered other institutions which allowed and encouraged voluntary helpers to engage in all kinds of tasks: household chores, decorating rooms, designing gadgets, writing letters, and performing such personal services as feeding and bathing. The view was taken that institutional life is enriched by this input from the outside world. Contacts with helpers may develop into personal friendships from which both parties derive satisfaction.

The Institutional Boundary: Excursions of Inmates

Where visitors are free to come and go in this way, it is also easier for inmates to go out; and moreover their excursions have a different quality. One establishment had a rota (maintained by an inmate) of volunteers who were willing to act as drivers and escorts for shopping expeditions or other events. Relationships that develop through helpers coming in to provide services can lead to invitations and outings. In such an institution it is more likely that invitations will be extended to inmates as individuals rather than as members of a category of cripples who are to be pitied. When inmates economize on the resources of transport and help by arranging group excursions, they generally choose public entertainments.

In a warehousing setting, where the boundaries are strictly regulated by staff, inmates go out less often, they are more likely to go out in batches, and they are also more likely to be taken to entertainments or classes that are specifically intended for the disabled. Thus the inmates remain undifferentiated from one another as passive recipients of recreational activities, and if an inmate asserts his individuality by making the only choice remaining to him – the choice of not joining the outing – he is labelled antisocial. A woman in one such institution considered herself very lucky to be permitted to go to church once a month on a Sunday evening; it meant that she did not get back until 8 p.m. and she was given to understand that this was very inconvenient for staff.

Differences between warehousing and horticultural institutions emerge in the holiday patterns of inmates (see *Table 21*). There is, however, less room here for individual variation. A disabled person who wishes to go abroad, for instance, must be prepared to pay not only for himself but for an escort as well. Hotels do not always provide accommodation for the severely handicapped; and few, if any, would accept incontinent guests. The disabled, therefore, may have little choice but to go to a holiday camp or hotel specifically set aside for them. Even so, it will be noted that in the two voluntary homes a higher proportion of inmates go on private holidays than on holidays arranged specifically for the disabled. The other three units show the opposite tendency.

TABLE 21 *Location of inmates' holidays*

Institution	Holidays for disabled	Own or parental home	Private holiday	No holiday	Insufficient information	Total*
VH 1	14	7	14	2	8	45
VH 2	6	6	7	4	—	23
LA 1	22	3	7	8	7	47
RHB 1	12	4	2	—	7	25
RHB 2	8	1	2	1	5	17
Total	62	21	32	15	27	157

* Some had more than one holiday in the previous twelve months.

Although we have emphasized the influence of the institution on inmates' contacts with the outside world, a factor of obvious importance is the individual's ability to move independently outside. Very few in our sample were, in fact, able to manage on their own. The highest proportion was in the local authority unit – about 20 per cent. In other units, only one or two were independently mobile. Those who move about inside the home with manually operated wheelchairs find it tiring to travel more

146

than a short distance outside. Kerbs and gradients defeat them. Even the minority with outdoor chairs or with electric three-wheelers are constrained either by the distance they can propel themselves or by the distance their vehicle can travel before the battery has to be charged. If an individual cannot transfer from his indoor to his outdoor chair without help this is a further constraint.

For the great majority, therefore, outings involve someone in the physical effort of moving inmates in and out of their chairs and in and out of vehicles. Special vehicles are often desirable, sometimes essential. If voluntary helpers are discouraged, the additional work devolves on staff, so it is scarcely surprising that excursions are less frequent; and this in turn further reinforces the pattern of maintaining staff control of the boundaries and of reducing opportunities for individuation.

Boundary Controls and Internal Relationships
As might be expected, just as the freedom of visitors to come and go tends to increase the frequency and individual quality of inmates' outings, so the total traffic of visitors and inmates across the boundary affects the internal life of the institution and, in particular, the relationships made within it, both between inmates and staff and among the inmates themselves.

Tight control of the boundary is, obviously, associated with a rigid, hierarchical distinction between 'carer' and 'cared-for' (usually designated 'patient'). Greater movement across the boundary tends to be associated with a more fluid, egalitarian relationship, in which the labels 'staff' and 'inmate' (or, more often, 'resident') refer more to a difference of role than to a difference of power and status. Within the former relationship, staff attach great importance to treating all inmates alike. To admit to personal preferences is to be unfair and unprofessional. Personal feelings are, so far as possible, suppressed. In the latter situation, as we saw in the last chapter, fairness is still a problem; but staff are much more likely to form friendships with some inmates and perhaps even spend off-duty time with them or accompany them on holiday. The difficulty in such an institution is to avoid discrimination against the 'cabbages' and isolates.

The correlation with relations among inmates is less immediately obvious. We found that greater openness in transactions across the boundary was associated with a higher quantity and quality of interaction. There were more interpersonal bonds between pairs of inmates and more friendship groups. And although some groups might be distinctly antipathetic to others, there was also a greater awareness of inmates as a total group. Needs of individual inmates tended to be more recognized and respected and there was more mutual help. A less incapacitated inmate would read to another, push a wheelchair, help with feeding. Even the simple act of lighting a cigarette for someone else displays awareness of other people's needs. It would seem that in the more repressive environments, with the pervasive culture of dependence upon staff, inmates are more likely to be in rivalry with one another for staff attention. Moreover, to the extent that staff have assumed control over the boundaries not only of the institution but also of the individual, both physically and psychologically, by a removal of choice even in physiological functioning, the inmate's personal identity is diminished. Being less sure of the boundary between self and other, he is less able to make and sustain interpersonal contacts.

Because even before admission the cripple has generally had less opportunity than others to assume multiple roles in the wider society, he has a strong proclivity within the institution to fall into and remain caught in his dependent role as a recipient of care. Consequently a powerful countervailing social system is needed to allow and encourage him to take up less passive roles. Benign permissiveness is not enough. This was evident in one institution in which staff were by no means repressive and could be described as *laissez faire* in their attitudes. Here initiative and independence were the preserve of a small group of the least physically handicapped, the incidence and quality of interpersonal relationships were relatively low, and the majority of inmates displayed, to a lesser or greater degree, the characteristic warehousing symptoms of withdrawal and apathy.

148

WORK AND WORK-SUBSTITUTES

In Chapter 6 we mentioned that it had been the hope of the founders of LA 1 that, in addition to catering for a severely disabled population, it would provide hostel accommodation for younger handicapped people who were still capable of holding down a job. This did not happen and at the time of our study only two inmates had jobs outside.

In all but a very few instances, inmates are almost by definition incapable of work outside the institution. For most, travelling to and from a place of work would present insuperable difficulties. Nor are the majority capable of the sustained effort required in a sheltered workshop, such as those operated by the Remploy organization. What, to the able-bodied, appears a simple task may require enormous effort from a person with muscular dystrophy. With the exception of a handful of gifted writers and artists, there is thus virtually no question of inmates earning their own living or reaching that degree of economic independence whereby they could pay for their place in an institution.

Work for the inmates generally, therefore, cannot be equated with work for the able-bodied, in that they will remain financially dependent whether they work or not. There is, nevertheless, a fairly widespread acknowledgement, explicit or implicit, of the importance of inmates undertaking some kind of work activity, and most are given the opportunity to do so.

Attitudes to work varied from one institution to another and from one inmate to another. We identified two different approaches to the question of work which we shall call the 'occupational therapy approach' and the 'work approach'. They correspond respectively to the warehousing and horticultural patterns.

The Occupational Therapy Approach

The warehousing institution, starting from the realistic assumption that inmates are no longer capable of a real work role, provides diversional activities, such as handicrafts, to give them something to do and to combat idle passivity. Apart from the actual physical experience of making an article, however, the inmate is still in a passive rather than active role. In effect, he exchanges dependence on a nurse for dependence on a therapist. Articles are made at the therapist's suggestion and usually sold by her at a modest profit. The inmate is not concerned with ordering raw materials or with finding a market for the finished product. He does not pay for the materials, he rarely buys or keeps what he makes, and he receives no payment for his work. Surpluses generally go into a welfare fund over which he has no control.

This approach is not confined to occupational therapy as such. It may underlie industrial outwork also. The crucial point is not whether the task is basket-making or light assembly work for a factory, but to what extent it gives inmates a role that is differentiated from that of psycho-physical dependency. In one institution, for example, a regular work centre was open daily; inmates were paid for their work and staff were employed to run the centre. Staff canvassed local firms for work, maintained liaison with them, collected raw materials, returned the finished product to them, and were responsible for the viability of the operation. Outwork had been chosen by the institution because it was hoped that inmates would find this activity more meaningful than handicrafts. It was argued that they could feel they were doing a real job of work which was of value to the community. The staff found, however, that although the majority of the inmates dutifully attended the centre for the stipulated three hours each morning, the job itself had little relevance for them. Inmates when asked about the work said that it was a means of passing the time. They did not see it as a job that related them to the community or as one that able-bodied people would have to undertake if they did not. Staff complained that inmates were interested only in the money and that most of them did not pull their weight. (Since all received the same amount – three shillings a day – regardless of individual or collective output, they were in effect being paid attendance money.) At times when there was a deadline for a particular job, and staff applied pressure on the ground that failure to meet contracts would result in the loss of future orders, inmates were resentful or apathetic. Staff then found that they had to finish the job themselves – and sometimes worked overtime to do so. Had the staff been a little less zealous in getting the job completed and instead encouraged inmates to take on some of the entrepreneurial responsibility or let them experience the consequences of failing to do so, this work centre might have moved in the direction of what we have called the work approach.

The Work Approach
The main characteristic of this second approach appeared to be inmate participation and involvement. In one rural institution where this model operated, the superintendent had, as in the previous example, built up contacts with local industry within a radius of some thirty miles, and inmates were again involved in light assembly work. A good deal of ingenuity was used to devise alternative money-making activities for those who were too badly handicapped to take part in the outwork: for example, an armless inmate operated a roadside produce stall on a self-service basis. Everyone was expected to do, and actually did, a full five-day week, for which he received £1. A further ten shillings a week was set aside and paid out as a twice-yearly bonus. All income received over and above inmates' wages was used to improve the amenities of the home. Inmates themselves put forward proposals and decided how the money should be spent. Work for them, therefore, meant not only additional pocket money but an opportunity to contribute financially to the home, and loss of earnings affected them not only individually but as a group. In other words, they found themselves being able to give instead of always receiving. Many had been in institutions all their lives. Under patient leadership, however, initiative and responsibility among inmates were gradually but significantly increasing.

In two other institutions, work was entirely organized by inmates with no staff assistance. One of them had had an occupational therapist when it was founded eight years previously, but she was removed at the request of the inmates and they took over. Inmates worked either as individuals or in small groups. In one instance, a percentage of the profit was ploughed back into the workshops and contributions were made towards the facilities of the home. The whole of the enterprise, from the ordering of raw materials to marketing and the allocation of profits, was carried out by inmates. Surpluses were used in a variety of ways: for example, to provide a TV set for a permanently bedridden inmate and to purchase a second-hand car for common use. However, it takes a sophisticated institution to allow members to earn differing amounts of money from their own independent enterprises and at the same time to contain others who, whether from choice or advanced infirmity, have opted out of such activity.

Some inmates who ran private businesses hoped that by this means they would build up sufficient funds to make it possible for them to leave the institution and support themselves in the outside world. Generally, however, proceeds were sufficient only to enable them at most to pay for a holiday abroad. The gap between earning, say, thirty shillings a week and the amount required to enable a person to live in a home of his own is practically unbridgeable.

Mr Newman is a person who has considered and regretfully rejected the idea of trying to cope on his own. At Mary Marlborough Lodge he stayed in a flat in order to judge whether or not he could cope outside an institutional setting; but the time and energy required to prepare a meal, for example, were such that he could not see himself managing without help. Mr Newman has tried a variety of jobs to supplement the social security benefit, including printing, hand-painting scarves, and colouring prints. An acute flare-up of his disability, however, may make him incapable of work for several months. Despite the time and energy he devotes to his job, the returns are pitifully inadequate.

But although Mr Newman and others have failed to achieve their hopes of 'complete independence', what they have found are roles through which they can express and sustain those parts of themselves that seek independence. Where the occupational therapy approach fails is in equating work with finding occupation for idle hands and, perhaps, providing some pocket money.

Allocation of earnings is indeed a major topic of debate in such settings and we have heard many arguments about the relative merits of paying the amounts involved (which are exiguous) on a flat rate to all, on a basis of individual output, or on a basis of individual effort. The point that is missed in these arguments is the sociological and psychological meanings of work and payment in the wider society. All too few workers derive much satisfaction from the actual tasks they perform, though they derive some from the social relations of the work-place. They are concerned less with the precise basis on which they are paid than with more generalized notions of equity (cf. Jaques, 1956 and 1961). Earnings are important for the opportunity they provide to take up other roles and engage in other activities as householder, parent, pigeon-fancier, and so forth. Expenditure involves the individual in choices and conflicts. It seems to follow, therefore, that while inmates' work can seldom be judged by the same criteria or confer the same status as work in the outside world, it should so far as possible simulate the meaning of 'real' work in terms of affording them the experience of a second role, through which to relate to the institution and to the environment, and of the choices and conflicts that go with it.

INMATES AND INSTITUTIONAL MANAGEMENT

For the able-bodied adult, the area in which he has the greatest opportunity to order his life and to make a multitude of decisions, ranging from the major to the trivial, is within his own home. All the institutions we studied were intended to provide their inmates with an alternative to geriatric wards or, in the local authority sector, to the former workhouses. Their founders started out with the view that physical disability was not synonymous with total helplessness or mental deficiency and they sought to create institutions which simulated an ordinary home environment and which gave residents the opportunity to live as normal a life as their disabilities permitted. These intentions are reflected in the formal statements of aims:

'A community where the young chronic sick can make a contribution.'

'A home, rather than a hospital, where patients are encouraged to take whatever part they can in the day-to-day running
of affairs.'

As we have seen, in some institutions the original intentions
are forgotten or receive only lip-service. Inmates are regarded
as incapable of making any contribution or any decision. Staff
take over, and even the more enterprising inmates, recognizing
their dependence on staff, learn quite quickly that attempts to
make decisions about their own lives will earn them only
opprobrium as trouble-makers. However, even in institutions
where the original principles still stand and the personal
liberties of inmates are valued, practical interpretation of the
ideals gives rise to a good deal of perplexity and ambivalence.

One problem is that, whereas in an ordinary household rights
and obligations are so built into the fabric of habit and convention that the family member is scarcely aware of observing
them, in an establishment ten or twenty times as large, these
tend to acquire the status of explicit rules. Staff perceive the
rules as necessary for the orderly running of the institution;
inmates resent them as infringements of personal freedom.

The locking of the building became an issue in one institution.
A recently appointed matron discovered that the main door
remained unlocked at night and asked the Management
Committee if it might be locked in the interests of general
security, and in particular for the sake of the night nurse.
Inmates resisted the locking of the door. They contended
that it played little part in security since would-be intruders
could find other means of entry. Their main opposition to
the proposal lay in their fear that staff would lock the door
at an early hour and that their own freedom to come and go
as they pleased would be curtailed. There were differences
of opinion as to what constituted a reasonable hour to lock
the door, staff suggesting 11 p.m. and inmates midnight.
Management Committee decided that the door should be
locked and that keys should be available to inmates and staff.
A month later the matter was again raised, this time by
inmates, who claimed that keys had not been produced. Staff

countered that it was too expensive to provide keys. Management Committee confirmed that a number of keys should be provided and left staff and residents to agree what time the door should be locked.

When they are given an opportunity to take some responsibility for managing their own lives and to participate in the running of the home, inmates sometimes fail to show the interest and gratitude expected of them. Instead they may appear to be lazy and apathetic and make demands on staff to do things for them. Staff, who have hoped for a genuine partnership, become discouraged.

One situation of this kind related to holiday transport. Inmates going on exchange visits to institutions in other parts of the country had been provided with free transport by the local authority. When this service was withdrawn, the Management Committee was requested to pay for transport. If this request was refused, the holidays that two of the inmates had already arranged would be in jeopardy. The Residents' Welfare Fund was quite substantial enough to meet the expenses if these two were otherwise unable to go; but the inmates claimed that their own fund should not be used for this purpose. They placed the onus on Management Committee, on the grounds that it was the Committee's policy 'to encourage residents to go on exchange holidays'. In the event, the Committee agreed to pay for transport for the holidays already arranged, but underlined that it was not thereby committed as to future policy.

At times, paradoxically, it may be a feeling of insecurity that causes inmates to retreat into an unreasonably dependent position. In the instance just cited, for example, the Residents' Welfare Fund had symbolic importance as something over which the inmates could exercise control; if it were diminished, the feeling of independence that it conferred was likely to be diminished too.

A not infrequent source of difficulty is that inmates' participation in the running of the home is interpreted in terms of their giving such help as they can with domestic tasks, keeping their rooms tidy, and so on. This could seem to be a perfectly reasonable interpretation so far as it goes; it tends to fall down when inmates aspire to do more than domestic chores (which in some cases they may be physically incapable of doing), while staff cannot accept that inmates should take on more influential roles.

In a small, informally run institution, the problem of how inmates can participate and contribute may solve itself. If the head of the institution consults inmates and takes their ideas and wishes into account before introducing any changes, they have in effect participated in decision-making while scarcely being aware of having done so. Difficulties may come, however, if the head is replaced by someone with different ideas and the informal consultative procedures lapse. In one such institution, now perceived by inmates and staff alike as providing a benign environment, one or two inmates are alert to their reliance for this state of affairs on the present leadership and to the potential disadvantages of a change.

Unless such an informal resolution emerges from intuitive qualities of leadership, aspirations of inmates to have a say in the running of 'their home' collide with staff authority. Staff legitimately say that they are employed to run the institution and to look after the inmates who are incapable of looking after themselves. Inmates, equally legitimately, assert that they are adults and have a right to manage their own lives. Staff are concerned about their moral and legal responsibilities. If an inmate insists on being up and about when a staff member, on medical grounds, believes he should be in bed, and if then the inmate dies, will not the staff member be held accountable by the coroner? In reality the legal picture is obscure. Inmates can justly counter that as adults they have the right to accept or reject medical advice. This was a perennial issue between successive matrons and the residents of Le Court. Finally it was agreed that a resident had the right to reject medical advice provided that by so doing he was not endangering the health of others (as in the case of infectious disease); but the matron could demand in return a signed statement to the effect that the resident accepted responsibility for the consequences of his decision.

The question of whether the inmates could call the institution 'their home' cropped up in a practical way early in our research. As a matter of course, when we wrote to request permission to visit an institution, we addressed our letter to what we believed to be the appropriate official concerned – superintendent, warden, matron, and so on. This official duly replied, usually in welcoming terms. Once or twice, however, when we subsequently talked to inmates, it was made very plain to us that they disapproved of having been committed, without consultation, to participation in our study.

At the time of our intervention at Le Court, the inmates' demand to share in the running of their home would be satisfied by nothing less than full representation on the Management Committee. They had already reached the stage of having their own participant observers present at Management Committee meetings – a prerogative of which by no means all the staff, or even all the inmates themselves, entirely approved. This was an institution in which inmates were exceptionally active, both internally and externally. Internally, they had a strong Residents' Welfare Committee and engaged in many tasks that elsewhere are the preserve of staff; and in external affairs, responsibility for public relations devolved at least as much on inmates as on Management Committee or staff. Why, then, were they not satisfied? In part this was a search for an issue on which to fight, which, as we have seen, is a facet of the horticultural defence. However, in so far as there are areas in which the rights of inmates do, in fact, conflict with the responsibilities of staff, the maintenance of some conflict between them will be constructive and healthy. While it may prove possible to reach working agreements, as on keys or medical advice, operation of these agreements needs to be closely monitored by both parties. For staff, such a relationship poses problems far beyond those of providing physical care and they find themselves in a role for which they are not trained. They may nevertheless derive satisfaction (albeit grudging satisfaction) from the liveliness of their charges. As for inmates, political activity of this kind, which brings them into the realm of serious adult decision-making, provides them with a second institutional role through which they can fully assert the active, independent aspect of themselves.

CHAPTER 9

Support:
The Unacknowledged Conversion Process

THE APPROPRIATE MODEL

All inmates have, and must have, a substantially passive role as recipients of physical care. They are the throughput of a system of activities designed to perform this task. We have argued that this task is most appropriately defined in terms of providing for psycho-physical dependency.

All inmates receive opportunities for at least some recreational and diversionary activities, which may have work-like characteristics. In some institutions this too is achieved by providing them with passive roles as the throughput of a system of activities set up for this purpose, perhaps under the leadership of an occupational therapist. In such a case this system is barely differentiated from the first. We have argued that this second task is most appropriately defined in terms of providing for psycho-physical independence. Its performance requires a second (but not secondary), separate system of activities, within which inmates themselves have roles as part of the resources of the system, not as its throughput. If the system is concerned with work, for example, the input may consist of raw materials and the output of finished products; inmates are the resources through which this process is achieved. The distinction is illustrated in *Figures 1-3*.

We have suggested further, however, that such a system fails to cater for psycho-physical independence unless the inmates also take on some responsibility for procurement of the raw materials, for disposal of the products, and for overall management of the system. In other words, they should take up roles in which they themselves manage certain transactions between the institution and its environment. In its most fully developed

158

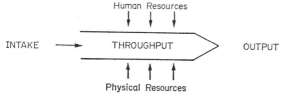

Figure 1   The general model of a system of activity

Figure 2   A system of activities for psycho-physical dependency (nursing care and occupational therapy): inmates as throughput

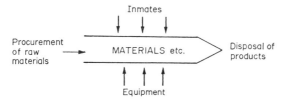

Figure 3   A system of activities for psycho-physical independence (work): inmates as resources

form this second system would give each individual at least one role that confers on him some independence in managing transactions across the boundary. He should at a minimum be a member of a group that takes on such a role. In general terms, this system is concerned with maximizing areas of discretion and opportunities for decision-making.

Since these two systems are engaged in divergent tasks, they are to some degree in conflict. Consequently, the individual inmate can be expected to experience some corresponding conflict between the roles he occupies in them. It is perhaps

159

worth reiterating our reasons for believing that such role conflict is appropriate.

The 'normal', able-bodied adult in our society carries a number of roles and is quite frequently in the position of having to reconcile the conflicting demands that these roles make upon him. There are, for example, the conflicting demands between work and family. Within each of these areas there is a number of potential 'sub-conflicts'. A married man, for example, may be subject to conflicting pressures from his wife, from his children, from his own family of origin, and from his wife's family of origin. Similarly, work may involve him in a set of roles within which his commitment to his employer pulls him in one direction and his commitment to his union in another; or, alternatively, if he is in a managerial post, he may have to find a way of mediating a variety of conflicting pressures from different sources – from his superiors, his colleagues, his subordinates, and, perhaps, his customers or clients. Indeed, the conflicting loyalties and role ambiguities of the individual in modern complex societies are often seen as a cause of breakdown in mental health (cf. Kahn *et al.*, 1964). It is nevertheless beginning to be recognized – for example, in cases of long-term unemployment – that absence of such conflict can also be a hazard to mental health in that it militates against the development and maintenance of a mature personality. It is here that the absence of opportunities for making decisions, even about relatively minor issues, is of considerable importance. Any decision, however minor, entails not only the adoption of one course of action but also the rejection of another. The rejected course of action must, at least in some measure, be felt as a loss.

The inmates of most institutions have little experience of this kind. Membership of the institution prescribes the dominant role as physical dependency – which in the warehousing setting extends to complete psycho-physical dependency. This, on the one hand, pre-empts the possibility of conflict with other roles and, on the other, entails delegation to the institution of many of the decisions that the able-bodied adult would have to make for himself. The resulting pattern of behaviour is not one that is likely to foster the development of a mature personality.

The only conflict left for the individual inmate may be the unreal conflict between what in fantasy he would like to be able to do if only he were able-bodied, and what in reality he is capable of doing.

This, then, is the argument for providing the inmate with opportunities to take up roles in two discrete and partly conflicting systems of activity. But while such provision may go a long way towards sustaining the inmate's identity as an adult individual, it is not enough merely to leave the options open in this way. The task of these institutions, as we defined it in Chapter 5, goes beyond this. Their intake consists of people who have been extruded from the wider society and for whom, by and large, there is no going back. In other words, the institutions import the socially dead and export the physically dead. *Thus the task must be, first, to help the individual to decide how he is going to make the transition from social to physical death; second, to provide him with opportunities to follow the route he chooses; and, third, to support him in implementing his decision.* He may choose dependence; he may choose hyper-activity; he may modify his choice as his physical condition changes. Both the choice and its sustained implementation, however, are so much more painful and difficult than the issues that ordinarily confront most of us that specific help and support should be made available for this purpose. Provision of support thus becomes a third conversion process.

In practical terms, this would imply specialized resources in the form, for example, of trained psychotherapists or counsellors either practising within the institution itself or, perhaps preferably, operating from their own independent bases outside. Their role would differ somewhat from that of their colleagues with more conventional practices in that they would have to operate with extremely limited therapeutic objectives. Notions of cure or rehabilitation, which imply leaving the institution, would seldom be appropriate. Correspondingly, they would need to treat their clients' personal defences with more than usual caution and respect.

Professional support of this kind was almost completely lacking in all the institutions we saw. We encountered only one institution that specifically catered for this role. Here a trained social worker spent half a day a week on the premises; and he was there to help with the solution of practical problems as well as more specifically to provide the kind of personal support for individuals with which we are concerned here. In one other institution, one or two inmates had occasional sessions with psychiatrists.

There is, of course, an acute shortage of professional workers capable of filling this role and cripples in institutions cannot claim high priority for such limited resources as there are. Even if one accepts this as a constraint, it is still pertinent to ask, especially in the light of frequent comments by staff about the psychopathology of their inmates, how effectively institutions deploy such resources as they have in providing personal support.

We shall see in this chapter that such support as there is is often tacit or even unintentional; that some potential sources of support are undermined; and also that in some institutions the primary task gets reversed, so that the objects of support are not the inmates but the staff.

CULTURAL SUPPORT

Every type of institution, however structured or informal, develops a culture within which certain kinds of behaviour are encouraged and others discouraged. Formal or informal sanctions reward conforming behaviour and punish deviant behaviour. For better or for worse, therefore, the institutional culture exerts a powerful influence on the inmates. The influence is supportive, however, only if the culture is congruent with the inmate's needs, in terms of the specific strategy he has chosen.

In institutions operating according to the warehousing ideology, dependency is the norm. The inmate is invited simply to hand himself over to the institution to be looked after. For inmates who have chosen dependency as their way of coping with the problems of progressive disability, such an institution might seem to provide a benign climate. One difficulty to which we have already alluded is that what is being encouraged in such institutions is not a mature dependency; the most favoured inmate may tend to be the most helpless. Conversely, in supporting the norm of dependency, such institutions implicitly, if not actively, discourage the individual who, while accepting the reality of the dependency, has the wish and ability to find positive outlets for his activities.

In institutions operating under the horticultural ideology, on the other hand, the norm is achievement. Selection procedures for admission tend to weed out the less active and more dependent candidates and to select those more likely to benefit from the particular milieu that the institution can provide. This again is appropriate for some people: for those who find difficulty in being 'self-starters' the cultural support for achievement can be substantial. Added support derives from the fact that in such institutions the norms are more likely to be set by the inmates themselves. Individuals' needs, however, do not always remain constant. The achievement culture can be highly supportive and constructive in the earlier stages of a progressive illness but perhaps less so later, when the individual ceases to become capable of achievement and has 'given up'. He may then appropriately prefer to lapse into a more dependent role and merely be looked after. In one horticultural institution, where the dominant culture among the inmates was achievement, a subgroup of staff conformed to the warehousing ideology and concentrated its attention on a highly infirm and dependent minority. This subgroup was split from and attacked by other staff and the majority of inmates: it was accused of trying to deprive inmates of their independence. Such splitting suggests some unreality in the assumptions made by both sides: inmates' capacities and needs do not have such either/or characteristics. Plainly the achievement culture did not fit everyone and could be sustained by the majority only if they denied their anxieties about utter dependency and projected them into the collusive subgroup.

In the local authority home we studied there were, as we saw in Chapter 6, very loose criteria for admission. The principal criterion was prior residence in the catchment area of the institution. Accordingly, inmates displayed an unusually wide variety of capacities and needs, and perhaps as a corollary of this there developed in the institution what might be called a *laissez faire* culture. Neither dependency nor achievement was actively encouraged; nor were they actively discouraged. The culture was permissive; but it was not supportive.

This indeed sums up the strength and shortcomings of cultural support *per se*: to be effective it must actively encourage certain kinds of behaviour and discourage others; but the more successfully it does this, the less able it is to cater for a wide range of individual needs or for the differing needs of the same individual over time.

RELIGIOUS SUPPORTS

Several of the institutions we saw were run by religious groups or had been founded by lay people with strong Christian convictions. Generally, applicants were accepted regardless of creed, and little pressure was applied to non-believers to attend services or conform to the prevailing beliefs. Only in one, in which all staff were required to be practising members of the Church of England, was participation expected (and obtained) from all inmates too. Our brief visit there gave us the impression that for the majority of inmates, if not for all, this was a significant source of personal reinforcement. Non-believers would probably find such a cultural environment unsupportive; just as a believer living in an institution that did not support him in his beliefs could find himself in difficulty.

An institution with a strong religious orientation is not necessarily better able to accept that its primary task is concerned with the transition from social to physical death, but at least it should be less likely than others to evade the problems of dying.

In our interviews with inmates, we respected their religious beliefs – as we respected their defences generally – and avoided probing. We can therefore only be tentative in our conclusions about the nature of the support they provide. The haunting question for every cripple is, of course, 'Why did it have to be me?' Certainly the Christian set of beliefs offered an answer satisfying to some. It enriched the life that remained to them and the use to which they put it. As we said in Chapter 3, there are universal myths about the cripple, which either relegate him as a pariah or elevate him to a saintly position, closer to God than the rest of mankind because of his physical impairment. These myths evidently have the function of allowing us to evade coming to terms with cripples as the people they are and discriminating between them. We have met a few who, supported by religious belief, seek meaning in their own experience and ways in which it may be applied to the benefit of fellow-cripples, other minority groups, and society at large. For others, religious faith offers the more conventional reassurance that their present stunted lives are only a preparation for a life after death.

While the Church operates at a cultural level in supporting the beliefs that individual inmates happen to have, it has failed to fill the vacuum we have mentioned at the level of individual counselling. There remains a need for trained workers who are able to help the individual inmate in his task of discovering the meaning of his own distorted life and his own personal strategy for dealing with his approaching death.

INTERPERSONAL SUPPORT

A growing child is not influenced directly by the culture of the society in which he grows up; this is mediated through his membership in a variety of institutions and, above all, in the family, which, with more or less effectiveness, reconciles the demands of the wider society and the idiosyncratic needs of the child. Similarly, the adult in coming to terms with the wider society has the support of close interpersonal relations, especially his membership of the marital pair. The work of the Institute of Marital Studies and others (Bannister *et al.*, 1955; Pincus, 1960; Bannister & Pincus, 1965; Dicks, 1967) has revealed the complexities of the collusive processes obtaining between husband and wife and has shown that, while in some cases the processes may be destructive, more often they are mutually enriching.

Of inmates who have ever been married at all, few retain

with the spouse a relationship that still has a supportive or enriching quality. Since the cultural supports, however, are either indiscriminate or ineffective, the need for support at the level of the interpersonal relationships is strong. The need is there even if the individual's mode of adjustment is consistent with the institutional culture; it is even greater if there is some inconsistency: as, for example, when an individual is struggling not to become submerged by the prevailing dependency in a warehousing institution. However, supportive pair relationships are seldom structured into the institutions we visited and, indeed, they are often discouraged.

Staff–Inmate

The nature of the support that staff can give to inmates is limited in one important respect: in every institution there is a rule implicit or explicit that no member of staff should have a close personal relationship with one inmate. The reasoning behind this is clear: the staff exist to serve the inmates collectively and for a staff member to give too much attention to one inmate deprives others to a greater or lesser degree. Even in institutions where by objective standards the staff–inmate ratio is generous the fact that the inmates are there because in some measure they have been rejected by the wider society almost inevitably means that subjectively staff are felt to be a scarce resource. In the study, we repeatedly came across examples of inmates using all sorts of means to capture more than what appeared to be their fair share of attention from staff. The methods could range from aggressively demanding behaviour at one extreme, to flattery and obsequiousness at the other. The rules against favouritism are sometimes gently enforced: for instance, the head of one institution reminded his staff that inevitably they would like some inmates more than others, but he requested them not to show it so clearly. In other institutions the social structure itself interposes such a barrier between staff and inmates that any intimate relations crossing this boundary are unthinkable. In one establishment in which the superiority of the nursing staff and the inferiority of the patients were defined with especial rigour, it was noted that kitchen staff insisted on having a different set of crockery and cutlery from that used by the patients: like untouchables in India, the patients were evidently perceived as polluting, and ritual measures had to be taken to protect the staff from them. One group of voluntary homes have written into their constitution that any staff member who marries an inmate is automatically to be dismissed. This again reflects the pervasive fear that close relationship between staff member and inmate will be destructive. Certainly in some institutions the stringency of the sanctions against the development of such relations suggests that there are strong, irrational elements at work. In other words, the fantasies about the consequences of such relationships are scarcely related to reality.

We have already discussed the extent to which such sanctions are functional for both parties where intimate bodily services are being provided. Sexual arousal in particular must be kept at bay in a heterosexual pair of which one member is dependent and the other must be dependable. We have also noted that long-term care magnifies both the need for such defences and the dysfunctional recourse to them. Depersonalization of the patient debases the quality of psycho-physical care. And where staff are rotated between inmates – another practice which has defensive connotations – attention varies in quality: inmates learn to welcome the ministrations of some and to dread others whose handling is rough or unsympathetic.

We wonder, in fact, whether the high professional standards of hospital nursing are justified in residential settings where the cost of the corresponding defence mechanisms is evidently so high. What happens when the defences do break down? We came across one particular instance in which a close attachment had developed between a female nursing attendant and a male inmate whose lower bowel she washed out for him daily. Our first reaction was to share the disgust of the superintendent of the institution, who discharged the attendant and classified the relationship as pathological. Perhaps it was; certain questions nevertheless seem worth posing: Was that relationship any more pathological than a number of marital relationships that both husband and wife find satisfying? In any case, is the wider social definition, of what is pathological and what is not, necessarily relevant to these institutions, which are partly outside the boundaries of society? May it not be that the more relevant criterion is whether the relationship is supportive?

Certainly, we do not underestimate the difficulty of a nurse or attendant in maintaining a supportive relationship that could be defined as mature and non-pathological. She must retain her professional standards and she must develop a relationship that respects the individuality both of the inmate and of herself. When it occurs, such a relationship can be mutually supportive and rewarding. It does require, however, both maturity in the individual and a supportive culture. Ben-David (1958) has pointed out the general problem for doctors and nurses of having to satisfy, on the one hand, the standards set by their professional colleagues and, on the other, the demands of their clients or patients. Where the warehousing culture predominates, the nurse or attendant who is felt to be most supportive by the inmates she looks after is usually denigrated by her professional colleagues as failing to reach appropriate standards of competence and efficiency. Correspondingly, the nurse who is competent by the standards of her professional colleagues is seldom found to be supportive by the inmates. In only one of the institutions we studied did we discover a culture that appeared to support the kind of mature relationship adumbrated here. There it was possible for an attendant to be respected as competent by her colleagues and as supportive by her patients.

By and large, therefore, the inmate does not receive specific and personal support in his relationships with staff. If he does, it is, as it were, only as one partner in a 'polygamous' relationship: he has to share the staff member's support with other inmates and to cope with his own feelings of rivalry towards them. Furthermore, unless the relationship has become, from the institutional point of view, pathological, it is not of course a relationship within which any sexual feelings can be overtly expressed.

Inmate–Inmate

At one level, inmates have a great deal in common. They share a common plight, in terms of their disabilities, their dependence, and their rejection by the wider society, as well as a common role within the institution itself. Collectively, they belong to the whole sub-society of the disabled. Many, or indeed most of them, read magazines written by the disabled for the disabled. Movements like the Disablement Income Group are thus able to mobilize a great deal of backing. Yet within the individual institution, although they share a common plight, inmates are also, as we have seen, forced into a position of competing with one another for the attention of scarce resources in the form of staff. The inmates of an institution can cohere most readily as a group in opposition to staff, but it is on staff that they depend for their physical care. Therefore they cannot afford to cohere too much. Without staff's help they would suffer acute discomfort and even die. Thus whenever in an institution there developes an 'anti-staff' group of inmates who protest about the standards of treatment and about the failure of the staff to recognize their individual needs, there also arises – indeed there must arise – another group of inmates who accept and support the way in which the staff go about their job. It follows that in any institution the inmates as a group provide only a modest amount of support of the individual in his task of coming to terms with his situation. Support must be derived from a relatively small subgroup of inmates or from a pair relationship.

We have pointed out that interpersonal relations between inmates are enhanced where there is greater involvement of inmates in external relationships. Even so, the number of inmates who apparently derive little or no support from their peers seems to be surprisingly high. Our evidence for this is subjective and impressionistic. If our observation is correct, however, it would accord wih sociological findings about 'total institutions' generally, as well as with our own other data about the problems for the inmate of establishing and maintaining an individual identity. The ideal member of any total institution, explicitly or by implication, has no private self, no secrets. In an article entitled 'Greedy organisations', for example, Coser (1967) has suggested that both the sexual promiscuity practised in certain closed religious communities in America and the celibacy of priests in the Catholic Church have an identical function in this respect: each device inhibits development of a close pair relationship which might stand in the way of the community's capacity to demand complete loyalty from the individual.

In the institutions we saw there were frequently strong pressures against the development of heterosexual pair relationships between inmates. Most institutions, as a matter of policy, rule out marriage between inmates: if it occurred, one or both would be required to leave. We found only one example of a cohabiting married couple in the establishments we studied. (There was another couple in an institution that we visited, but they were allowed to meet only in the public rooms.) The strong implication was that marriage and the mutual support that the marital pair provides were the preserve of the able-bodied and incompatible with institutional life. Sometimes we were told that the disabled were incapable of close, emotional relationships: emotionally, they were too shallow. All sorts of obstacles were put in the way of the development of such relationships. In some cases, quite stringent steps were taken to segregate the men from the women: they were not allowed into one another's rooms, for example. To some staff, even the notion that cripples might have sexual fantasies, let alone perform the sexual act, was felt to be obscene and disgusting. (The widespread taboo on marriage within the institution suggests that such unions are the equivalent of incestuous relationships and arouse a corresponding horror.)

Even apparently sophisticated heads of institutions found various rationalizations to justify marriage as a bar to continuing residence and the controls they exercised to prevent sexual relations from developing. One argument often used was that in the absence of control there would be a large number of unwanted babies, perhaps themselves cripples too, who would be a charge upon the institution. Contraception, sterilization, and abortion were evidently not considered to be adequate protection against such an eventuality. The fact that some disabled couples would find it physically extremely difficult, if not impossible, to have sexual intercourse at all was not taken as a reason for being more permissive; on the contrary, there would be rather ribald speculation about the difficulty that a spastic couple would find in copulating and about the help of a third party that they might require.

In addition, therefore, to policies discouraging marriage and to physical controls exercised to prevent a couple from having the opportunity of being alone together, more subtle controls were applied in most institutions to denigrate the whole notion of a mature heterosexual relationship developing between inmates. The net effect was that the maturity of such relationships was devalued, and in a climate that expected them to be superficial and ephemeral they were, in fact, often superficial and ephemeral. Moreover, it was not only staff who were non-supportive of such relationships; residents colluded in the same set of values. The envy of those inmates who were unable to develop such a relationship may well have obtruded into the attempts of those who were struggling to do so. Inmates themselves then tended to take on the value system that suggests that marriage, or a mature heterosexual relationship without the legal tie, is the preserve of the able-bodied.

Consciously or unconsciously, therefore, strong pressures are applied both by staff and by residents to inhibit the establishment of a close pairing relationship or, if such a relationship is established, to break it up.

Inmate–Outsider

The third potential source of support is from the relationship of an inmate with an able-bodied outsider. Where they develop, such relationships can be beneficial both to the individual inmate involved and to the institution at large. We have noted that in some institutions voluntary helpers are kept at arm's length, so that personal ties are unlikely to develop at all. Greater opportunities for such relationships tend to be accompanied by greater anxiety on the part of the head of the institution about his responsibility for the development of a pathological liaison. Understandably, there may be a fear, say, that a middle-aged male friend may exploit a young female inmate, even if she is over 21.

This problem of responsibility is enormously complex, and

171

there are no simple solutions. For example, although the inmate may be over 21, she will, as a result of living in an institution, have had a diminished opportunity for exercising judgement and choice and is therefore likely to be immature. To intervene will be to persist in impairing her personal development; yet not to do so may produce a situation that she will regret. One liberal argument is that the lives of inmates are so impoverished that if they can gain some enjoyment from sexual adventures they should be encouraged rather than the reverse. Against this, however, it can be argued that advocacy of one morality for the cripple and another for the able-bodied is discriminating. Although these issues are often debated by staff, it is notable that the dilemmas are seldom shared with the inmates themselves. Experience in Le Court suggests that such sharing can sometimes lead to acceptable policies which, by defining the boundaries of responsibility between staff and inmates, are supportive to both. Undefined boundaries in this area can in themselves make it more difficult for inmates to establish external relationships and to manage them sensibly.

It has to be recognized that most close relationships between an inmate and an able-bodied outsider will contain some collusive elements which might easily be interpreted as pathological. In other words, in return for the support the inmate receives in his disability, he must reciprocate by giving some form of support that the outsider needs for his own disabilities or deficiencies of a different kind. It is notable that many of the voluntary helpers at residential institutions (like many of the staff too) themselves have some handicap or have a handicapped member in their family. While we found many instances in which this complementarity could be mutually beneficial, the fact remains that only a minority of inmates of the institutions we studied had a viable interpersonal relationship with an able-bodied outsider.

The general point to be made, therefore, is that not only does the institution fail to provide the inmate with supportive relationships, particularly heterosexual pair relationships, but in general it actively inhibits the development of any relationship that might prove to be supportive.

172

DISTORTION OF THE PRIMARY TASK

Indeed, far from providing support for individual inmates, some institutions appear to be set up in such a way that their primary task is to provide support for staff. The inmates are a means to this end.

We had repeated evidence that staff vacancies in residential institutions attract candidates who, while not having a visible physical handicap, are, in some measure, socially handicapped themselves. For instance, the proportion of divorced or separated staff members in these institutions almost certainly exceeds the proportion in the population at large. We did not check the medical history of staff, but a large number of cases were brought to our attention in which the individual had a history of mental illness, often involving treatment in a psychiatric hospital. One institution in particular had made it a policy to recruit staff who would find it difficult to secure employment in other occupations, including explicitly schizophrenics and epileptics. The institution was seen as providing a suitably sheltered environment for them. While it may be convenient for the wider society to kill two birds with one stone in this way, it is scarcely conducive to providing for the needs of the physically disabled, who are the *raison d'être* of these institutions.

Collusion between the helper and the helped, of course, always exists. The mother needs the baby; the nurse cannot exist without a patient to be cared for; the psychiatrist has a vested interest in mental illness. To be effective in such roles, the individual must make use of personality characteristics that in other settings might well be diagnosed as pathological. Generally speaking, however, society is alert to the dangers of these collusiveprocesses. Thus, the demands of school and the new relationships that it provides wean the child from all but the most possessive mother. Again, we have recently seen the public debate about heart transplants and the concern that the over-enthusiasm of surgeons or heart patients should not lead to a situation in which some potential donors become more valuable to society dead than alive. These residential institutions, however, as recipients of individuals whom society has

already rejected, are less amenable to the processes of wider
social control and there is thus a greater opportunity for collusive processes to develop that are more destructive of the
inmate's individuality than supportive to him.

One form of insurance that an institution can adopt to prevent
such distortion of its primary task is to recruit to its staff people
who have an established role in the wider society – for example,
women with families of their own outside – and who do not
depend for their personal identity and social status on maintaining superiority over the people in their care.

CHAPTER 10

Export Processes

COPING WITH DEATH

We argued, in Chapter 5, that these residential institutions as a class are confronted with the unique and intractable problem that inmates once admitted are unlikely ever to be restored again to the wider society. With few exceptions, the inmate will be in one or other institution until he dies.

Every human institution, of course, can expect to lose some of its members by death. In some hazardous occupations, where the statistical probability of someone getting killed is appreciable, rituals and other defence mechanisms are structured into the relevant institutions to prepare for this eventuality: colliery towns and parachute regiments are examples. A still more obvious example is the hospital, which is much more geared to death than most. Even so, of the patients who are admitted to hospital, far more leave as convalescents than as corpses. An institution in which, in one sense, the problem of death is inescapable is the family. There again the significant outputs of the family are the children who become the parents of the next generation and, in the normal course of events, death comes to the individual only after he has fulfilled his roles as spouse, parent, grandparent, and, in the case of a man, breadwinner. Moreover, the family in modern society is increasingly inclined to hand over its problems of death to other institutions; thus it is the hospital that has to deal with the terminal stages of an illness.

In all these instances, therefore, death is the exception; it is an unhappy by-product, so to speak, of performing the institution's primary task. Hospitals, for example, are primarily devoted to curing their patients. From this standpoint a death is a failure of the system. Every effort is made to prevent or postpone it. In such a culture, to die is to be a failure. On these

grounds it is questionable whether the hospital is ideally equipped to deal with terminal care as a psycho-physical problem.

Closer to the institutions we are concerned with are the
monastery and the old people's home. In both, the usual
expectation is that the entrant will remain there until he dies,
barring serious illness for which the resources of the institution
are inadequate. In the monastery, however, the decision to
enter has been made voluntarily and the option of leaving,
though it may not be exercised, always ultimately exists; and
in the case of the old people's home the entrant has usually
lived out most of his life in what society would regard as an
acceptable and productive series of roles.

What characterizes the institutions we are concerned with
here and makes them different from any other type is a combination of three factors:

(i) admission may be at a relatively early age, so that the span
between entering and dying may be very long indeed;
(ii) entrants have either never experienced a range of acceptable and productive roles in the wider society or, if they have
had such experience, it has been prematurely cut short; and,
(iii) admission for the most part is involuntary and there is
often nowhere else to go.

It is difficult, both for the inmates and for those who look
after them, to come to terms with these realities. The problem
is least (though that does not mean it is inconsiderable) for those
who have had polio and for institutions in which such people
constitute the majority of inmates. Once the disease has struck,
the individual is in a position to assess what aspects of functioning have been lost and what remain to him, and to plan, with
little more uncertainty than most people, what he will do with
the remainder of his life. The person with a progressive disease
is much more vulnerable: he faces gradual, usually step-wise
decline in capacity. Although the decline itself is predictable,
the rate at which it will occur is not. Static periods, during which
the progress of the illness is arrested, may be short or long:
they cannot be planned for. Of the inmates in this category
whom we interviewed, only a minority seemed able to face the

future and prepare themselves for it. One woman, for example, was able to say that the next problem she would have to face was incontinence; a man with muscular dystrophy was aware that he had aready survived beyond the expected time-span and that a sudden bad cold could prove fatal. We met one or two others who were deeply depressed, said they would welcome death, and resented being kept alive. Many other inmates, however, found it impossible to look realistically into the future: they were buoyed up by fantasies in which staff tended to collude by offering unsubstantial reassurances.

> Mr Oliver's wife had got divorced from him because of his multiple sclerosis. His condition was deteriorating and he would need permanent and increasing institutional care. His expressed hope was that he would find another woman to marry him, take him out, and look after him.

> Mr Pepperd was in an RHB unit and had the same illness. His ambition was transfer to another hospital where he would receive the proper treatment and recover.

In institutions that retain their inmates until death, the death-rate may be between 10 and 20 per cent a year. But even though the reality is there to be examined, it appears to receive surprisingly little attention either from inmates or from staff. So far as we could detect, the death of an inmate is not used by others as a basis for considering their own problems about their future or lack of it.

When an inmate is dying, often the response overtly aroused in others is less one of sympathy than of resentment. Resentment springs partly, no doubt, from the unwelcome reminder of mortality. It seems also to be linked to the extent to which the dying person is perceived as attracting an unfair share of staff attention; the others feel relatively left out and rejected. Resentment may be accentuated if the dying person is not in a single room; the others complain about the noise made by the patient or by those attending him.

The death, when it occurs, seems to receive scant attention. Staff in these institutions have frequently commented to us on the lack of grief displayed by fellow-inmates when one of their number dies. Staff themselves, for that matter, appear to show little grief. The absence of grief and mourning indicates perhaps the social irrelevance of most inmates in these institutions. It is an exceptional person indeed who is recalled for very long after he has died.

Descriptions we have received of what happens when someone dies suggest that death brings with it some release of tension in the institution. This applies whether or not the terminal phase has been protracted. The phenomenon may well be comparable to the process that has been observed in, for example, parachute regiments or airlines when an accident occurs. In such circumstances there is grief, of course, but there is also a release of tension because the fatality has happened – 'and it wasn't me'.

Although staff with whom we discussed this problem of death appeared to be able to acknowledge that in many instances it was a happy release, the conventional attitude that life is of itself valuable, whatever the content of living, is very pervasive. One nurse, describing the death of an inmate whose kidney function had failed, said:

'We kept her going for a whole month; it's not kind, but we have to.'

Nurses in warehousing institutions showed pride in their resuscitation procedures. A common viewpoint was that the painful feelings aroused by death had to be kept at bay:

'In hospitals you are taught to feel detached and then you don't feel the tragedy of a person dying, for example.'

The more insightful staff were able to recognize that much of the strain inherent in their work arose from the fact that inmates were incurable and that the institution therefore somehow had to cope with the reality of death. And the strain is made greater by the general evasion of this reality in our society. The head of one unit, who had served in it for ten years, grieved at the deterioration of so many of her charges – people of whom she had become very fond. 'There's so much death around', she said; and the care she could give them seemed so inadequate, yet there was nothing else she could do.

When society insists that homes for incurables should be happy places, it is hardly surprising that those responsible for running them should feel that they have failed when their actual experience is so different. The real failure is in shying away from acknowledgement that it is a central task of the institution to help its inmates to find a way of dying. The difficulty that able-bodied members of the wider society have in facing their own mortality encourages denial that this is the task. Yet we believe that the institution that learns to manage terminal care and becomes a good place to die in will be a better place to live in.

DEFENCE MECHANISMS: SURROGATE EXPORTS

To work or live in an institution that has little hope of effecting any positive change in its 'throughput', who can leave only by dying, and that has no control over its 'exports', in that death is uncontrollable, is inevitably painful, both for staff and for inmates. In earlier chapters we have considered some of the defence mechanisms that are used to avoid facing these realities. Here we examine specifically the defences that affect the export system.

One defence, to which we alluded briefly in the last chapter, involves a denial that death is a significant ending. Religious beliefs have a defensive connotation if they are used to discount the relevance of life on earth and to redefine the task of the institution as one of preparing its inmates for the life hereafter. To paraphrase, instead of serving as an export system from mortal life, the institution is seen as the import system of immortal life.

Other types of defence, on which we shall be concentrating here, involve a denial that the primary task of the institution is to secure the transition of inmates from social death to physical death; some other kind of output is sought instead.

Transfer before Death

One strategy – implicit rather than explicit – is to try to avoid situations in which inmates die on the premises. As we saw earlier, some establishments have striven to do this by setting an upper age-limit after which inmates would be transferred to a geriatric institution. Although explicitly set up to cater for a younger age-group, they have often, in the event, found it difficult to implement this policy and been under considerable pressure to retain their inmates to the end. Those that set themselves up as sheltered workshops have good reasons for trying to find alternative accommodation for inmates who are no longer capable of making use of the facilities provided. One or two of the institutions we visited defended themselves from the problem of deterioration and death by asserting that they could not provide the staff necessary to cope with incontinence or illness generally. Some, too, have a low tolerance of any deterioration in mental health: any inmate who shows signs of disturbance is rapidly transferred elsewhere. In such cases, the staff do not always find it possible to tell the remaining inmates the truth about what has happened. 'He has gone away on holiday' was the fiction in one institution run by a religious order, and we were told that the remaining inmates usually did not question the explanation. Perhaps they did not because they dared not.

Thus many cripples who have initially experienced rejection from the wider society, by being put into an institution, are faced with a further rejection in the later stages of their life. While we recognize the magnitude of the problems involved, we cannot believe that an institution in which the staff are unable to tolerate deterioration and death is one to which incurable cripples should be admitted. Such an environment not only provides no support; it actively promotes feelings of insecurity.

Fantasies of Rehabilitation

Another common mechanism of defence against the problems of death is to pretend that death is the exception rather than the rule. In many of the institutions we visited, fantasies were promoted both by staff and by inmates that they were concerned with processes of cure and rehabilitation. In other words, the 'normal' output would consist of people restored to full roles in the society outside.

There is always a sufficient basis of fact to support such fantasies. For example, when a cripple is assigned to an institution after the death of fond and over-protective parents it may transpire that he is not quite so helpless as he and his parents have tended to believe; institutional care is then seen as having effected an improvement. All sorts of special aids can be made available to enable individuals to do things for themselves that they did not think they were capable of doing; with the result that it becomes possible for them to contemplate a life with some semblance of normality in a specially equipped flat outside. Occasionally this becomes a reality. Again, a personable young man may find a warm-hearted able-bodied woman to marry him and take him out to look after. A great deal of publicity, both within the institution and outside, tends to be given to those who do find their way back to the wider society[1] – much more publicity than to those who die – and consequently it becomes the more credible to believe that death is the exceptional way of ending one's stay in an institution. Apart from developments in prosthetic appliances and so forth, advances in medical science itself encourage the hope that the disease of today may have a cure tomorrow.

Where staff and inmates alike collude in supporting such fantasies it becomes, of course, correspondingly more difficult for inmates to find support for the reality that most of them will, in fact, have to face.

Dilution of Outputs

Two institutions that retained almost all their inmates until death also incorporated secondary units catering for patients convalescing after serious operations. This may be interpreted as a means of trying to dilute the proportion of the inmate population who left by dying. The care of such patients, in whom they can watch steady signs of improvement, provides a welcome contrast and relief for staff who otherwise are dealing with nothing but deterioration, no matter what they do. When

[1] A series of BBC television programmes in 1968 featured a woman heavily crippled with arthritis who, after many years in the geriatric ward of a hospital, succeeded in finding a council flat and a companion to look after her in it.

such systems were set up, it appears to have been hoped that the incurables would gain some comfort from seeing improvements in the convalescents. This hope seems ill founded. In one institution it was found that the convalescents preferred to dissociate themselves completely from the incurables, whom they regarded as virtually untouchable; obversely, there seems to have been some resentment on the part of the incurables of those who were able to escape.

One or two institutions adopt an opposite strategy: they take in for terminal nursing a few patients who are dying of, say, cancer. Their presence is expected to make the longer-stay inmates feel grateful and relatively fortunate. However, without in any way stigmatizing the staff who grapple with the great difficulties of terminal care, we must consider the possibility that they are using this as a diversion from the even more demanding primary task of helping those who will never get better but will take much longer to die.

Staff as the Alternative Output

A further defence mechanism is operated to a greater or lesser degree in all the institutions that we studied: most behave as if the critical import–export process is not of inmates but of staff.

Now it is clear that in institutions in which the majority of inmates stay until they die, the turnover of staff will be higher than the turnover of inmates. Moreover, the dependence of the inmates adds to the relative power of the staff. An anomalous situation characteristically arises, therefore, in that the staff who are transient can have a substantial effect in modifying the norms, the values – indeed the whole culture – of an institution in which the residents are relatively permanent (Higgins, 1963). The wastage of staff is high – over 30 per cent a year – though this is comparable with the wastage in other types of residential establishment. However, the Williams Report notes that heads of homes for the physically handicapped show a larger turnover than the heads of any others (National Council of Social Service, 1967, p. 87). Realistically, then, the comings and going of senior staff in particular are a matter of considerable concern to inmates.

A further relevant factor is the substantial strain of working in these institutions. Voluntary helpers, for example, who perhaps spend one day a week in an institution, have reported to us their feeling at the end of the day of being completely wrung out. Even among those full-time staff who have made residential care their profession, there is a particular strain involved in working among the physically handicapped and chronic sick. This is almost certainly attributable to the relative or absolute hopelessness of the future of these inmates. Staff, if they are good at their job, mop up the strain and may find it difficult to 'recharge' themselves at a rate that corresponds to the rate at which they are being 'discharged' by the inmates. We spoke earlier of the advantages of staff living out; they can then recharge themselves through their other roles in the community. For those who live in it is much more difficult and some respond to the strain by turning it back upon the inmates themselves.

These factors combine to provide a basis for a convenient and widespread mechanism of defence in which the staff, as it were, become surrogate exports. In every institution, there are one or more members of staff who are, or at least are seen by the inmates as being, incompetent, unsympathetic, or even sadistic. A process of splitting occurs, whereby these are contrasted with other members of staff, who are seen as competent and benign. When individuals become cast in such a role, the behaviour of the surrounding social system tends to confirm it even more strongly in them, so that the good are always seen as more virtuous than they are in reality and correspondingly the bad as more wicked. Every institution, therefore, develops a set of myths, particularly among the inmates. How wonderful it would be if only X could be removed. How lucky we are to have such a kind matron – if only the night sister weren't such a bitch. And there is always the myth of the golden age which is fostered by the processes of deterioration that take place in the inmates: memories of a benign matron in the past, who is contrasted with the ruthless and authoritarian woman holding the role at the present, are plainly sometimes an oblique reference to the individual's own experience of, in the past, being able to do more, feeling better, experiencing less pain. The process of myth-making has a potency of its own; splitting and projection take place not only in fantasy but in reality. The notion, 'If only we could get rid of matron', gets translated into processes of seeking support among members of staff or management who might be expected to subscribe to the view that the matron is less than adequate. The matron will become progressively more isolated or else will gather a small coterie around her in opposition to another, perhaps larger, group of staff and inmates who, as a result of the splitting itself, find her behaviour increasingly intolerable. If such people are watching for her to make mistakes they will find them. In a number of instances, we have seen a great deal of tension build up in this way around certain individuals. All that is bad gets projected into them. Eventually, either they leave of their own volition under the pressure or steps are taken to secure their dismissal.

The underlying fantasy is that when one has got rid of the delinquent member of staff, not only will the institution as a whole become a happier place to live in, but each individual will, in some way, be a healthier person. The leaving staff member, in other words, becomes a scapegoat.

Just as the incompetence and wickedness of the departing staff member will have been greatly exaggerated so, correspondingly, will the positive expectations of the replacement. With the new matron will come the millennium. She has all the virtues of dependability, tolerance, and devotion to the inmates. Since no human being can live up to such godlike virtues, the fall from grace must sooner or later follow.[1] When the new matron turns out to be not an archangel but only a human being after all, very often the mood swings back from canonization to scapegoating and the process starts all over again.

The persistence and pervasiveness of this kind of process must be related to its effectiveness in providing a distraction from the reality of the step-wise decline of so many inmates. We have indirect evidence to suggest that the euphoria that occurs when a hated staff member departs can be experienced

[1] See Bion's discussion of what he calls the dependent leader of a basic assumption group (Bion, 1961, pp. 78-86).

by inmates as a real improvement in health. For example, this is how one inmate described the response of another after the news that a hated matron was leaving:

'P, who had withdrawn completely, has suddenly and dramatically started talking to everybody and bothering about her appearance. I shouldn't be a bit surprised if she starts going down to meals again now.'

Correspondingly, the departure of a benign staff member, or a period of uncertainty during staff changes, may, it appears, be accompanied by a significant increase in minor illness and possibly also in the institutional death-rate.

Discussion of this particular defence mechanism cannot be completed without discussion of its obverse – the scapegoating of inmates by staff. Again, this appears to be related to the difficulty of tolerating the reality that a home for incurables, dealing as it is with the problems of deterioration and death, cannot, ultimately, be a happy home. Staff may tend to develop a belief that if only X would leave then the rest of the inmates would be happy. Other inmates may collude. X will be a trouble-maker, emotionally disturbed, depressed – in general, a bad influence. Sometimes ways are found of actually getting rid of X: he may be consigned to a mental hospital, for example. One superintendent told us about a situation in which there appeared to him to be two trouble-makers, one of whom he finally managed to transfer to another institution. Within a few months, this ex-inmate was dead. The tragedy, as this superintendent described it, was the discovery that they had got rid of the wrong person and it was the other inmate that they should have transferred. The point is that – as with staff so with inmates – the problem lies within the institution itself and the task it is there to carry out. It is a fantasy to believe that problems are located within an individual and that, if the individual leaves, the problems will go too. The 'badness' that he was taken as representing belongs uniquely and inescapably to each of the individuals left behind.

By the same token, it would be a mistake to be too critical of these defence mechanisms and to slip into the belief that, if

185

only one could get rid of these mechanisms and confront reality, the institution would spontaneously become a more satisfactory place to live in. Anyone who belongs to one of these institutions, whether as an inmate or as a member of staff, needs his defences and is entitled to preserve them. One must therefore be content with the much more limited hope that some members of staff will be able to transfer a little of their energies from the support of their defences – particularly those, like scapegoating, that have destructive consequences for individuals – to the provision of a little extra support for inmates in facing the realities of the situation they are in.

VOLUNTARY MOBILITY BETWEEN INSTITUTIONS

Transfers between institutions are relatively rare. Sometimes, as we have just mentioned, they occur when one institution uses another as a receptacle for a trouble-maker. We came across only isolated instances of inmates securing transfers for themselves. This was either to move nearer to relatives or in the hope that the new institution would offer a more benign environment.

In one sense, this kind of mobility can be seen as yet another institutional defence against coming to terms with death: it provides an alternative output. In so far as different institutions are operated in such markedly different ways, however, there are rational arguments for giving inmates greater opportunity to choose the one that best fits their needs and to move from one to another. Holiday exchange visits, which occur on a limited basis between Cheshire Homes, for example, provide scope for discovering what other institutions are like – and perhaps evidence for deciding that one is lucky (relatively) to be where one is. They are also one means whereby ideas from one institution are injected into another, thus potentially leading to improved standards. For both these reasons such exchanges could usefully be increased.

Some advocates of a national disability pension take the argument a step further and suggest that if the cripple received a pension and paid the institution to look after him, he would enjoy a higher status analogous to that of a guest in a hotel. He would be able to insist on a higher standard of care and the more custodial establishments would gradually lose their business to others that were more progressive in outlook. Attractive though this argument is, it has one snag: hotels reserve the right to evict awkward guests. If they are to cater for the needs of their clientele, these institutions should provide security of tenure. Yet it seems almost inevitable that greater assertion of inmates' right to leave would be accompanied by greater assertion of managements' right to expel.

CHAPTER II

Organization and Leadership

In this chapter we try to examine more precisely the implications for organization and for leadership of the model of residential care that we have been developing. We start from the point that the three 'conversion' tasks identified in Chapters 7-9 require three corresponding systems of activity. Organization is the means through which these activities are carried out and related to each other and to the external environment. We therefore suggest an appropriate organizational model and discuss the leadership roles, for the parts and for the whole institution, that follow from it. We go on to examine and evaluate the way in which these roles were actually distributed in the institutions we studied.

AN ORGANIZATIONAL MODEL

In Chapter 1 we postulated that any enterprise could be regarded as an open system, which takes in inputs from its environment and secures a pay-off by transforming them into outputs. An enterprise has many types of throughput and engages in a corresponding variety of import–conversion–export processes; the dominant throughput and the conversion processes that it undergoes are determined by the primary task.

There is no doubt that the dominant inputs of the kind of residential institution we are studying are cripples in need of care; but as we saw in the last chapter it is unrealistic to assume that its outputs should be cripples who have benefited from the care and been restored to the society outside. In this respect, the residential institutions we are describing differ fundamentally from most other enterprises with a human throughput. The modal outputs of a hospital are cured patients (though some die); of a college, graduates (though some fail or drop out on the way); of an airline, passengers who have

188

reached their destination (though a few miscarry). The modal outputs of the residential institutions with which we are concerned, however, are dead inmates; those who leave in other ways are exceptions. We have suggested that the inexorableness of the boundary at the output end of the system gives rise to many of the problems that are encountered both in running institutions of this kind and in living in them; and in particular it leads to difficulty in agreeing upon their primary task.

Since the primary task cannot appropriately be defined in terms of exporting rehabilitated inmates to the external world, then the quality of living within the institution must be an end in itself. We have, therefore, argued that it is 'the task of the institution, without either destroying the inmate's individuality or denying his dependence, to provide a setting in which he can find his own best way of relating to the external world and to himself' (p. 90). And the institution must at the same time accept the reality that the inmate is likely to remain in it for the duration of his life and recognize that the individual's anxieties about deterioration and death must also be a major concern of the institution.

Three systems of activity are required to carry out this task: these cater respectively for psycho-physical dependence, psycho-physical independence, and support. The system as a whole and the three constituent systems are depicted in *Figure 4*. The individual inmate occupies roles in these systems of activities and the arrows in *Figure 4* are intended to illustrate the point that from hour to hour the inmate may be continually moving from a role in one system to a role in another. All his activities as a member of the institution derive from his roles in one or other of these systems.

Each of the systems has a distinctive task and a distinctive method of task performance. It therefore requires its own management. The task of the institution as a whole is carried out by relating the activities of these systems to each other and to the environment. Thus, overall management of the institution cannot be contained within the management of any one of the systems: it must be external to them. The basic

189

organizational model is shown in *Figure 5*.[1] Institutional management is depicted as straddling the boundary of the institution and the outside world; the management of each constituent system straddles the boundary between that system and the rest of the institution.

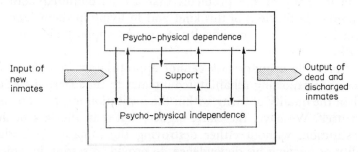

Figure 4   The institution as an open system, showing constituent systems of activities

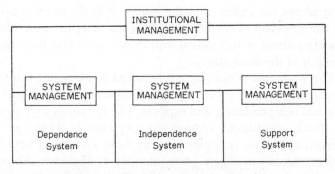

Figure 5   The basic organizational model

Figure 5 is a relatively abstract and simplified representation of systems of activities and of management roles. It offers a way of thinking about the organization of institutions which is substantially different from the 'official' forms of organization we have actually seen in use. However, it is still some way short of being a guide to the alternatives that may exist in practice. For example, an individual might take more than

[1] This topological representation of organization was developed by A. K. Rice: see Rice (1963, pp. 16-25) and Miller & Rice (1967, pp. 33-42).

one of the managerial roles shown in the diagram and a role might be carried by more than one individual. Such options may become clearer as we examine each of these systems in relation to the others and the leadership functions that are required.[1]

ORGANIZATION FOR DEPENDENCE

The system for psycho-physical dependence is the easiest to think about in conventional terms. It is here that are located the physical resources of accommodation, food, medical supplies, and so on, and the human resources of caring, catering, and cleaning staff, through which the activities of providing physical care are carried out. Inmates in their dependent roles are the throughput of this system. To take a trivial example from one of the many sub-systems of activity: the input may be an inmate needing a bath, the conversion process consists of bathing him or helping him to bath himself, and the output is a clean inmate. Virtually all these sub-systems are directed towards providing the inmates with help in their daily living activities – dressing, bathing, feeding, going to the lavatory, moving from place to place – together with occasional nursing in times of illness.

---

[1] 'Leadership' and 'management' are overlapping concepts. In distinguishing between them we follow the usage of A. K. Rice:

'At the level of manifest behaviour a leader has to be able to carry his followers with him, to inspire them, to make decisions, and to communicate them effectively to others; a manager has to get the best results out of the resources he has available – money, time, materials, and people. To be successful he has to display qualities of leadership. Nevertheless, some people are clearly better at leading enterprises and institutions than they are at managing them; others may be better administrators, or "managers" in the narrower meaning of the title, than they are inspirational leaders. In other words, while leading is not necessarily synonymous with office-holding, there can be no clear boundaries between them at the manifest level, and any enterprise whose managers do not give leadership in primary task performance is in obvious difficulty. But leadership can also be exercised unconsciously, and at this level "management", which for me has an essentially rational connotation, cannot be applied. Moreover, "manager" and "management" tend to be used more in industry and commerce than in other kinds of institutions. For these reasons I have used "leader" and "leadership" in discussing the concepts.

For theoretical purposes it is irrelevant whether leadership, or management, is exercised by an individual or by a group' (Rice, 1963, p. 15, footnote).

See also Rice (1965, pp. 20-3).

Difficulty arises, however, if this system is regarded as coterminous with the institution as a whole. It is, as we have seen, an assumption that is too readily made. Cripples are admitted to these institutions because they are incapable of fending for themselves and it is inferred that the institution exists to satisfy their dependent needs and only those needs. It is this that produces the warehousing model. Not only is management of the total institution undifferentiated from management of the dependence system; but because the other systems shown in our model are suppressed, the individual as an independent being has no room for existence and so management of the individual inmates' boundaries – their ego-functioning – is also taken over by the institution. The apathy and listlessness endemic in a warehousing institution arise from the fact that once the inmate has been 'processed' through one of the dependence sub-systems – for example, he has been converted from an inmate needing a bath into an inmate who has been bathed – there is no other role in another system into which he can move. He can only wait to become the input of a further dependence sub-system, through which he will be dressed, fed, dosed, given occupational therapy, and put to bed.

In our model, the dependence organization provides for only one set of roles and occupies only a part of the inmate's life-space. Between moving out of one dependence sub-system – as the bathed inmate – and moving into another – as the inmate needing to be fed – the inmate has to be able to leave the dependence system entirely and take up a different role within a different system – that concerned with psycho-physical independence. The recognized existence of such an alternative system is essential if the warehousing model is to be avoided. Inmates have to be able to move across a boundary beyond which they are outside the control and care of the dependence organization. Unless this possibility exists, there can be no support for staff in their mature management of the dependent relationship: the organization itself fosters the fantasy that staff are omnipotent and inmates totally dependent and it is is highly difficult for either party to find a more realistic mode of relating to the other. We are not, of course, implying by this that recognition of an alternative system makes it easy to avoid the collusion of unrealistic dependency. As we pointed out in Chapter 3, there is a tendency for the cripple to regress to an infantile dependency which invites a corresponding maternal omnipotence. But at least this type of regression is less difficult to control if both parties have the organizational evidence that their mutual interdependence is not an exclusive relationship.

ORGANIZATION FOR INDEPENDENCE

Here we move into an area which is organizationally more elusive: usually it is either labelled 'informal organization' or given no recognition at all. It is our contention that if the institution is to perform its overall primary task, it must create and foster a system of activities whose primary task is to provide opportunities for inmates to satisfy their needs as independent individuals.

A simple example of such a system of activities would be a factory run and staffed by inmates. If this factory were in a separate building, the inmate's change of role, as he moved from the dependence system to the independence system, would be marked by the crossing of a physical boundary. It is, of course, highly unlikely that such a factory would satisfy the independence needs of all the inmates or indeed all the needs of any inmate. Multiple sub-systems of activity are required for performance of this task. Some, like the factory, may be readily identifiable as 'work' – for example, a group of inmates who operate a typing–duplicating bureau, or a person who paints and sells pictures. Others might readily be discounted as trivial activities or pastimes if they were not recognized as being carried out within the context of an organization for independence – for example, arrangement of outings, or internal delivery of mail and newspapers.

Where a strong Residents' Committee already exists, it may be well suited to take responsibility for this task. Participation in the work of the committee itself provides significant roles. Where no such nucleus is available, it may be necessary at first for a staff member to lead this system. His job would be to make himself redundant as soon as possible. Earlier, we mentioned a group of inmates who asked that an occupational therapist should be removed once they had developed the necessary skills to run their workshop themselves and to train newcomers. One could go further and suggest that an inmate-led system might appropriately want to employ one or two able-bodied staff to provide specialized resources.

We said in Chapter 8 that inmates' work roles should expose them to crises and conflicts in their relations to the institution and to the environment. It is an important part of the experience of the independent role that the individual, either on his own behalf or as representative of a group of inmates, should engage in transactions with, for example, external suppliers or customers. Ultimately, however, a system concerned with psycho-physical independence cannot fully perform its task unless it provides some roles from which inmates can represent the institution as a whole. There are at least three ways through which this can be done. One is to provide opportunities for inmates to engage in such activities as fund-raising for the institution. (We would distinguish this from fund-raising by and for a Residents' Welfare Committee. Institutional funds might perhaps be devoted to residents' welfare, but the decisions on their expenditure are made by institutional management.) A second is to establish a consultative system, through which inmates' views can influence the formulation and implementation of the institution's policies. A third way is to permit inmates to take roles in institutional management itself, which we discuss below. Although only a very small number may be both willing and able to take such roles, it is important that the opportunities should exist and be perceived as existing.

In one sense it may be misleading to talk of a system with the task of providing for psycho-physical independence, for it is plain that in the sub-systems of activities that arise inmates, like any other members of work organizations, will be expressing and satisfying their dependent as well as their independent needs. Correspondingly, of course, within the caring system, which is concerned with providing for psycho-physical dependence, there will also be activities in which the inmates are

194

expressing their independence. What is important is that the primary tasks of the two systems are fundamentally different and that the institution gives organizational (and also cultural) acknowledgement of the need for both.

The horticultural model, with its over-emphasis on achievement, is a reaction against domination of the dependence system. It is concerned with anti-dependence rather than independence. It rests on a belief (no doubt partly justified) that the institution is dominated by the dependency system. Through it, inmates are able to use the institutional structure defensively: if the inmate projects into the structure his problems of psycho-physical dependence he can avoid having to confront them and come to terms with them within himself. If the institution manifestly caters for both dependence and independence this defence is less readily available.

ORGANIZATION FOR SUPPORT

The model that we are developing here for a residential institution for the handicapped has something in common with a university. The university offers the undergraduate dependent roles in the teaching and residential systems; and, partly through project work in the teaching system and partly through an array of student-led activities, it also offers him independent roles. The educational process is carried out through the student's movement from role to role in these systems. Universities also recognize, explicitly or implicitly, that they are engaged in a maturational task – they are converting schoolboys into adults – and that undergraduates may need support in navigating their way through these systems, in dealing with problems of identity and in planning future careers. Some universities organize a tutorial system around this need; almost all nowadays provide a student counselling service.

Inmates of these institutions, too, require support in somewhat similar problems. In its most developed form this might in fact be given through an internal 'tutorial' or counselling service, backed up by external psychiatric resources. Mental health is at risk in these institutions and preventive work is required. It is not enough to wait for signs of acute disturbance; continuous pastoral work is much more to the point, with a constant watch on the pathogenic characteristics of the institution itself. Indeed, because institutions inherently have such characteristics, it is desirable that leadership of the support system should have strong external backing and thus some degree of independence. A possibly useful model is the type of industrial medical officer who concerns himself with the health of the enterprise (cf. Bridger, Miller & O'Dwyer, 1964): he is sufficiently involved in the enterprise to understand its commercial constraints and at the same time professionally independent enough to be critical.

Shortage of funds and indeed of the relevant professional skills will in practice make only modest solutions possible – for example, more intensive use of church and other voluntary community services. By including 'support' in our model we are mainly concerned to emphasize that this is something that needs to be thought about and organized: it should not be left to chance.

INSTITUTIONAL LEADERSHIP

We define the primary task of leadership as the management of relations between parts of the institution and the whole, and between the whole and the environment, in such a way as to obtain performance of the primary task of the institution.

In discussing leadership of the institution we shall initially, for simplicity, speak of this role as if it were filled by a single individual. In practice, it may be occupied by more than one person. Thus leadership may be distributed between a paid official (such as a matron) and a voluntary group (such as a Management Committee); and sometimes inmates may take on aspects of the leadership role. Subsequently, we shall want to consider these important variations. We conclude, however, that if, as in most instances, there has to be a full-time 'head of the institution', he must have sufficient authority to discharge his responsibilities effectively.

Internal relations will plainly be affected by the extent to

196

which the leader is able to control the boundaries with the outside world; we therefore start by looking at these boundaries.

Legitimation

In whatever way an institution defines its task, the leader has to secure acceptance of, more precisely, legitimation of, that definition from the wider society on which it depends for the resources through which the task can be carried out and also for the supply of inmates who are to be looked after. Bodies running voluntary homes raise money from the public at large, both locally and nationally, and in many cases also receive financial support for their inmates from local authorities and, if they can be registered as nursing homes, from Regional Hospital Boards. Thus in these cases a variety of 'publics' have to be satisfied on a continuing basis both about the aims of the institution and about its capacity to carry them out. Units operated directly by local authorities or by RHBs differ from voluntary homes in this respect: the process of legitimation has been largely worked through by the time these units have been first inaugurated, and thereafter it can generally be taken for granted unless there is a major change in external policy or internally in the way in which the institution carries out its task.

The process of legitimation carries with it a number of constraints. Registration as a nursing home, for example, involves an undertaking to employ a stipulated minimum quota of qualified nursing staff. Other constraints are much less explicit. Often, for example, it seems that when a voluntary body extracts a contribution from a member of the public, it is making a tacit bargain that it will take over the problem of the incurables and encapsulate them within institutions removed from society. The generous donor may well be the first to protest when there are proposals to convert the house next door into residential accommodation for them. He is saying, in effect: 'I will give you money if you will take them away and look after them; but keep them out of my sight.' Many families part with their crippled members on the same basis as donors part with their money: they are asking the institution to take over full responsibility.

Indeed, in the case of units run by local authorities and RHBs, it is often considered that it is part of a citizen's rights to have his disabled kin cared for by 'the authorities'.

The nature of these tacit bargains places strong pressures on the leadership of the institution to operate it according to the warehousing ideology. 'The authorities' are to be dependable custodians; the inmates are to be dependent and to show gratitude by appearing to be happy, but they must not obtrude.

Public opinion is slowly changing in this respect, partly as a result of pressure groups of the disabled themselves, and it is an aim of this book to help to promote such a change. Even so, the leader whose definition of the primary task is at variance with the implicit warehousing definition faces a constant struggle for legitimation, especially in the local community. Most people in the community do not wish to be reminded overmuch of the cripples in its midst. Cripples are not automatically welcomed in shops and cafés, pubs and clubs. In a few cases, nevertheless, heads of institutions operating the horticultural ideology have battled successfully to gain the acceptance of their inmates within the local community on the basis of: 'they are just as normal as we are'.

Leadership of this kind, which brings the institution into a more direct relationship with the local community, is plainly healthier than the other type which accepts conventional prejudices and does not press too hard. However, it still falls short of what we would regard as the appropriate and even more difficult task of the leader, which is to present the reality of the situation to the community and to foster a relationship between the institution and the community on the basis of this reality. Otherwise there is the risk of presenting a stereotype of inmates that is over-determined by community prejudice or by the fantasies of inmates themselves.

The reality is that inmates are in some respects like the able-bodied but in other respects they are not. Differences arise from their physical dependence and the psychological mechanisms they use to cope with this; from their financial dependence; and, more generally, from their lack of opportunities to fill the multiple roles that are available to most members of the society

198

outside. Moreover, all inmates are not alike. While some are undoubtedly brave and happy, others are anxious, depressed, and in pain; some are intelligent, others are unintelligent or, almost as awkward, find verbal communication difficult or impossible. Some inmates are really making full use of the capacities that remain to them; others may have opted for a more dependent, withdrawn role as a means of coping with their condition. Therefore, as long as the leader, in his attempts to relate the institution to the community, presents the inmates in a stereotyped way, whether this be as contented wards or as striving individuals, he is constructing its relationship with the community on a false foundation. This, in its turn, necessitates and fosters the use of the social defence mechanisms within the institution to keep reality at bay. Only if the leader can succeed in building the external relationship on a basis of reality, which is concerned not with accepting or with denying, but with examining the nature of the differences between the able-bodied and the disabled inmates, is it going to be possible internally to build up a structure and a culture that are appropriate to the institutional task as we have defined it. It then becomes feasible to develop with the community a relationship which, though still dependent, is not parasitically dependent, in the sense that inmates are not demanding that their status entitles them either to preferential treatment or to equal treatment. The relationship is less stereotyped and more diversified. We were struck by one case in which a rural institution ran a conventional fête for fund-raising but, unconventionally, the inmates donated the proceeds to the village church restoration fund. This small shift from the usual taking role to the giving role appeared to have a positive effect on community attitudes towards the institution, as well as to enhance the inmates' self-esteem.

Admission and Discharge

If the institution is doing its job of accommodating inmates for life it can exert no control over its 'export' boundary, which is defined by death. If it discharges them before this, it is failing in its task. The leader requires correspondingly greater control over the admission boundary. Unless he can determine and enforce criteria of admission there will be a mis-match of inmates' needs and institutional resources, the internal systems of activities will lack a stable relationship with each other, and task performance will be jeopardized. As we pointed out in Chapter 6, the imposition of criteria need not imply 'skimming the cream'; it might even involve rejection of all candidates who are not in the most urgent need of residential care. Whatever the criteria, to the extent that there is some homogeneity in the characteristics of the input, it becomes more possible to create an internal structure and culture within which the differing needs of individual inmates can be recognized and met. Excessive heterogeneity in the input, on the other hand, seems to lead to the institutional imposition of a spurious homogeneity – in fact, a homogenization – which denies and destroys individual differences.

Control of Internal Boundaries

Internally, leadership is required to ensure that the activities of the constituent systems are carried out in relation to each other in such a way as to obtain performance of the overall primary task. The most important aspect of this is to maintain the separate integrity of the dependence and independence systems and a clear boundary between them. Movement of the inmate from one role to another is otherwise impossible.

However, this is also difficult to achieve. Dependence of the institution on the wider society promotes a dependent culture internally. This can readily preclude anything else and lead to the collusive 'basic assumption dependency' behaviour described by Bion (1961), in which inmates express only dependent needs, staff exist only to satisfy them, and it is the role of the leader to be an omnipotent source of succour to all. Correspondingly, the leader who shows himself to be anything less than completely infallible is discarded. Underlying and reinforcing such behaviour may be a fantasy that the leader is potentially capable of curing the incurable. Such collusion becomes a little easier to resist if leadership of the whole institution and leadership of the part concerned with dependency are recognized as

200

separate roles and assigned to different people. The separation, however, is apt to be accompanied by primitive splitting processes, whereby the overall leader is preserved as a benign figure and the badness is projected into the person in charge of the caring activities.

Again, it is difficult to build up a second system of activities around the positive task of independence. Anti-dependence is more readily mobilized. The latter is related to another kind of basic assumption behaviour – in Bion's terms, 'basic assumption fight/flight' – in which the inmates are united in fighting against or fleeing from an external enemy, who is again likely to be the head of the caring system. Anti-dependence is inimical to genuine independence, since it involves inmates in participation at a primitive emotional level and not as mature, ratiocinating individuals.

No leader can prevent the social structure from being used in this way as a defence mechanism. Inmates and staff will inevitably try to deal with some of their internal conflicts by projecting them into the structure. In this respect members of residential establishments differ from members of any other organization only in degree: their problems over dependency are more intense. But whereas most people outside belong to multiple social systems between which they can, so to speak, distribute their projections, these inmates and many of the staff have only the one: it is a total institution. It is this that generates such strong collusive pressures to settle for a warehousing model or a horticultural model – structures that meet the defensive needs but inhibit task performance. Therefore even if the values of the external society were more congruent with the task we have defined, the structure through which it is carried out would still be precarious, since it encourages the examination of conflict – especially intrapersonal conflict – rather than the avoidance of it. So long as the constituent systems of activity are performing their task, there will, for example, be occasions when the staff of the dependence system will be under fire for fostering undue dependency and failing to relinquish inmates to their independent roles, and other occasions when the staff will allege that inmates' independent activities are jeopardizing their health. The institution could not be alive if such conflicts did not arise. When he is called upon to adjudicate on the boundaries of the two systems of activity, what the leader has to resist is the temptation to take over and erode the ego-functioning of others by making their decisions for them and resolving their internal conflicts for them. Indeed, it is probably an important function of the leader to serve as a model, both for inmates and for staff, of a person who clings to reality, and who does not need to use the institutional structure as a means of dealing with his own internal conflicts.

THE DISTRIBUTION OF LEADERSHIP FUNCTIONS

We have spoken of 'leadership' as a boundary role which relates what goes on inside an institution to the wider environment. We have noted that this role may be occupied by one individual or, more usually, by a variety of individuals and groups at different times and for different purposes. We have identified the three principal functions of the overall leadership role in these institutions as:

(a) external legitimation of the institution, which may include fund-raising;
(b) management of the import or admissions system; and
(c) control of boundaries between systems within the institution.

Each of these constituent systems requires its own leadership role:

(a) management of the caring system;
(b) management of the 'independence' system; and
(c) management of the support system.

There was a good deal of variation in the allocation of these roles in the institutions we studied. In all five institutions, the function of external legitimation was wholly or mainly in the hands of an unpaid committee. In all five also there was a full-time head (superintendent, warden, matron, or sister-in-charge) who was responsible for at least internal coordination.

One significant difference between the institutions, already discussed in Chapter 6, was whether or not the full-time head was involved with admissions. A second point of difference was in whether or not the overall head was also in direct charge of the caring system. Third, they differed in the involvement of inmates in leadership functions: in the two institutions in which a system concerned with psycho-physical independence could be identified at all, its leadership was in the hands of an inmate group. The patterns are summarized in *Table 22*.

In the two RHB units the distribution of leadership functions was broadly similar. Each of the Hospital Management Com-

TABLE 22   *Distribution of leadership functions in the five institutions*

Functions of leadership	VH 1	VH 2	LA 1	RHB 1	RHB 2
(a) of overall institution:					
Legitima-tion	MC Inmates Warden*	MC	Welf. Ctee CWO	HMC Cons.	HMC Cons.
Admission	MC Cons. MO Warden Matron	MC Cons. S-i-c	Welfare Dept.	Cons.	Cons.
Internal boundary control	MC Warden	S-i-c	Supt.	Matron	(Cons.) Sister
(b) of constituent systems:					
Caring system	Matron	S-i-c	Supt. Sister	Matron	Sister
'Independ-ence' system	Inmates	Inmates	—	—	—
Support system	—	?S-i-c	—	—	—

Abbreviations:
HMC: Hospital Management Committee   MO: Medical Officer
MC: Management Committee   CWO: Chief Welfare Officer
Cons.: Consultant   S-i-c: Sister-in-charge
* The warden moved into this function in the course of our work with VH 1.

mittees had other responsibilities apart from the unit in question – which in the case of RHB 2 was a relatively small ward in a large hospital. Accordingly the consultant was involved in pressing the case with the HMC for the special needs of the unit. But in both instances the consultants themselves, who were specialists in geriatric medicine, had much wider responsibilities, within which the unit was a relatively minor preoccupation. Both nevertheless took sole responsibility for deciding on admissions and they also exercised general supervision over the running of the unit. Both the matron in RHB 1 and the sister in RHB 2 combined the functions of overall internal coordination and of management of the caring system. But there was an important difference. Whereas RHB 1 was physically and administratively a separate establishment, under a resident matron, the boundary between RHB 2 and the rest of the hospital was much more diffuse. Much of the administrative work was carried out at hospital level, which meant that there was little or no distinction in practice between the sister's functions in internal coordination and in management of the caring system; and, moreover, the sister and her staff were interchangeable with other wards in the hospital, with the result that it was the consultant himself who provided continuity in internal leadership. In both instances there were awkward ambiguities in the relationship between the consultant and the matron or sister. Formally, of course, the matron or sister was not accountable to the consultant: each reported through separate hierarchies to the HMC. Thus, although in each case the concept of the unit was the consultant's and he could greatly influence its internal life through his authority to decide on who should be admitted, internally his formal authority was limited to the medical care of individual inmates; his position did not entitle him to prescribe how the unit should be run, however much he might wish to do so. In RHB 1 this led to perpetual tension between the consultant and the matron. In RHB 2, nursing staff mobility left the consultant with greater *de facto* authority; but his other commitments prevented him from converting this into effective internal leadership. Given the limited and uncertain authority of those in charge of the day-to-day running of

204

these units, and in the absence of any distinction between the roles of head of the institution and of management of the caring system, the warehousing culture in each of these institutions seems to be an inevitable outcome.

In the case of the local authority unit (LA 1), the Welfare Committee and the chief welfare officer were relatively remote from the establishment, which was only one of many institutions and projects for which they were responsible. Admission, as we have seen, was effectively in the hands of the relevant local welfare officers; the resident superintendent had little or no say in it. He himself was directly accountable to the chief welfare officer for operation of the establishment within the budget that was determined for it. In practice the superintendent was also the head of the caring system. Although a non-resident sister was responsible for the activities of physical care, the superintendent took charge of the catering (and at one stage, when they were without a cook, did most of the cooking himself). Like the two RHB units, LA 1 had no discernible system of activity concerned with independence or support.

Legitimation is a more central activity for a voluntary home, which usually has to rely on its own fund-raising efforts for capital projects and often for meeting a deficit on income-expenditure account. In RHB and local authority establishments, donations pay for the extras rather than for the essentials; and fewer voluntary helpers are found, partly because the need for their services is less acute. Each voluntary home in our sample had its own Management Committee and in each case some members devoted a great deal of their time and effort to the needs of the institution.

In VH 2, a relatively small unit with only twenty-one inmates, a non-resident sister-in-charge combined some of the overall leadership functions with management of the caring system. She had a great deal of freedom to run the unit her own way. A House Committee, consisting of representatives of Management Committee, voluntary helpers, and inmates, confined its attention to such matters as buildings, furniture, and equipment. An Admissions Subcommittee of the Management Committee, together with a medical consultant, was involved in the selection procedure, but since an assessment holiday at the institution was an integral part of the procedure, the sister-in-charge had a determining influence on the constitution of the waiting-list; and she also effectively decided who should be taken from the waiting-list to fill a vacancy. Partly perhaps because the establishment was small enough to allow her to have a personal relationship with each inmate, she had little difficulty in reconciling her own leadership of the caring system with inmates' leadership of what was, in effect, an 'independence' system. Through these personal relationships she also operated an embryonic support system. This appeared to be the only institution in which it was recognized by senior staff that some attempt should be made to monitor and to try to meet individual inmates' needs for support.

VH I (Le Court) was not the largest institution at the time we collected our statistical data, but in the later phases of our study it grew to be so and correspondingly it had the most developed structure. Also, although the inmates in VH 2 had no less influence on institutional policies and their implementation, inmates' influence in VH I was much more formalized. Representatives elected by the Residents' Welfare Committee became almost full members of the Management Committee.[1] (Elected staff representatives had similar roles but less effective power.) Inmates were active in raising funds for institutional as well as for Welfare Committee purposes. Internally, leadership of the caring system was in the hands of a matron. As in VH 2, an inmate-led 'independence' system was emerging but had not yet attained explicit organizational recognition. The full-time head of the institution was a warden. At the time we began our collaboration with Le Court, the warden had little authority and in his internal boundary control function he was reinforced by the chairman of Management Committee and by a House and Finance Subcommittee. We helped in redesigning the role of warden, as a result of which outside members of Management Committee were able to withdraw from day-to-

[1] Subsequently, inmate representatives were appointed to the Admissions Subcommittee of Management Committee and also to a new subcommittee responsible for the recruitment and selection of senior staff.

day intervention, while the warden himself became a more active representative of the institution in transactions with the environment. It would appear that this has helped the institution to move a little beyond the anti-dependence of the horticultural model towards a culture in which both dependence and independence can be acknowledged and provided for.

Evidence from this small sample supports the hypothesis that the role of the full-time head of the institution has a crucial effect on its culture. It is notable that in the three institutions (RHB 1, RHB 2, and LA 1) where the head has no effective authority to control the external boundaries with the environment, internally the caring system and the dependent culture predominate. It is as if his or her authority is so precarious that it would be threatened by any assertion of independence by the inmates. In VH 1 and VH 2, on the other hand, the warden and sister-in-charge respectively exercise authority on behalf of the institution in transactions with the environment. This transactional authority is associated with acceptance or encouragement of inmates' independent activities.

However, this is not the whole story. In addition to the fact that their external status was a function not merely of the titles they had but of the authority they exercised in those roles, both the warden and the sister-in-charge lived outside the institution and so had other roles in the community. This made it the less likely that they would be reliant on the dependence of inmates to bolster their status and personal identity. On the contrary, each of them, by having a foothold both in the community and in the institution, was better able to serve as the reality-based model, mentioned earlier, of a person who does not rely upon the institutional structure to resolve his internal conflicts, and better able too to provide personal support to staff and to inmates.

A further interrelated factor is, of course, the personal maturity that the head of an institution brings to his role. Transactional authority and the availability of other roles in the community help to maintain maturity and to reduce the likelihood of regression and collusion, but they cannot of themselves make the head of the institution into a mature person. This point is particularly relevant to VH 2, where the sister-in-charge was both head of the institution and head of the caring system – a combination of roles that gave her considerable power. There was no structural safeguard against her abusing her power. She did not do so because she was mature enough not to need to; but this was certainly a situation vulnerable to abuse by a less able successor.

Finally, we would suggest that the pressures in residential work with incurables are such that even the mature individual with transactional authority and roots in the community is himself at times going to need support. A further condition for effectiveness is that the Management Committee – whether it includes inmates or consists wholly of outsiders – should be prepared to withstand the inherent pressures towards institutionalization, to reject the simplification of a 'happy home', and to work persistently at more difficult, more demanding, and more constructive approaches to institutional care.

PART III

Implications
and Conclusions

CHAPTER 12

Some Immediate Possibilities

The work on which this book is based was called a pilot study. It has the shortcomings of drawing upon a very small sample and is open to the criticism of over-generalizing from inadequate evidence. Our obvious course at this juncture would be to recommend further research, through which our findings might be confirmed and modified.

A particular gap that some readers will have noticed is that although we set out to discover whether it was possible to create a more benign psychosocial environment in these residential institutions, we have not offered any way of measuring 'benignness'. For example, it would be satisfying if we could produce 'before' and 'after' indices to demonstrate that the inmates of Le Court had 'improved' as a result of our intervention there. But what are the criteria of 'improvement' in this context? When we were asked during our study what our own criteria were, we had difficulty in answering. We were not satisfied by notions of 'happiness', which for us could have connotations of passivity. The subjective comparisons we found ourselves making when we visited institutions had more to do with a quality of 'aliveness'. In some establishments, inmates were probing their environment, questioning assumptions, using their capacities. In many others, the inmates seemed to be inhabiting a shrunken world; the majority were moribund. Possibly one could devise an objective scale of aliveness, derived perhaps from a combination of observed behaviour and clinical interviews. However, this would not exonerate us from making value judgements: policy-makers would still have to decide whether more alive institutions are better institutions. For this reason, we have offered our own definition of the primary task of these institutions – a definition that reveals our own particular values – and we have described the organization required to perform this task. We have used our research findings to illustrate the problems that are likely to arise in attempts to implement the model we propose. More research is indeed required, but not as the next step. First, those responsible for managing the institutions have to decide whether our concept of residential care is one that they endorse. If they do, they have to initiate experimental changes to implement this concept. The research task is then the systematic examination of the experiences of changes in a variety of settings and the dissemination of the lessons learnt.

In this chapter, we consider changes that are within the scope of existing institutions and of the bodies that support and service them. In the next, we turn to the wider implications for national provision for the disabled.

RE-EXAMINATION OF TASK AND ORGANIZATION

Human institutions must satisfy certain needs of the people who staff them if they are to continue to survive. Unless there are strong countervailing pressures from the environment, satisfaction of these internal needs will tend to assume priority over the task that the institution exists to perform. Thus in many universities the provision of opportunities for research and career development for faculty has taken priority over the task of teaching undergraduates. Students can and do protest vociferously if they feel that their own needs are being subordinated to those of staff; but for a human throughput that is more dependent on the institution, protest is much more difficult. A correspondingly greater onus falls on institutional management to undertake frequent appraisals of what it is trying to achieve, whether its organization and staffing are appropriate to its task, and how far it is actually attaining its objectives. We have no illusions about the difficulties of such an appraisal, for it essentially calls upon the individual to confront his own ambivalences, to examine the discrepancies between his professed attitudes and his behaviour, and to try to distinguish reason from rationalization. Yet it is surely incumbent upon those who have responsibility for the lives of others to make the attempt.

In a few of the institutions we saw, the warehousing ideology is so pervasive that change is unlikely. In many others, those in managerial and staff positions express a desire to do a better job but go on to list the constraints that make this impossible. The reality of such constraints needs rigorous examination: many will prove after all to be not beyond the control of the institution.

It is commonly argued, for example, that inmates are so damaged, psychologically as well as physically, that they are incapable of moving beyond the dependent role. Attempts may even have been made to encourage their greater independence, but without success. We accept that most institutions have a few inmates who are irretrievably locked in dependency. But we have also observed that under patient and persistent leadership heavily disabled and institutionalized inmates can begin to move into independent roles. The institutional environment can be enriched; a greater variety of choices can be made available.

Similarly, the quality and availability of staff may constitute a real constraint; but the organizational and cultural setting in which they work can affect their performance substantially. The organizational model presented in the last chapter, for example, distinguished the role of head of the institution from that of head of the caring system. Where these two roles have to be occupied by one individual, the dependency culture is more likely to pervade the institution and he or she will require unusual qualities if a system of independent activities is to be allowed to develop.

It is relevant here to discuss the debate over the appropriate size for an institution. We are often asked our opinion concerning the optimum number of inmates. Smaller units are commonly said to be preferable because they permit greater attention to individual needs; on the other hand, it can be countered that the larger units offer greater variety and choice of relationships. In fact, size cannot be evaluated in isolation from organizational, cultural, and personal factors. The advantages of the small unit with twenty or so inmates can be exploited only if the institutional head has the appropriate concept of the task and the personal attributes to go with it. In the large unit of forty or more, where leadership of the caring system is likely to be differentiated, the head of the institution must have considerable managerial skills to create, and to help inmates to use, opportunities for multiple roles and relationships. Potentially, the most vulnerable units from the point of view of size may be those with between twenty-five and thirty-five inmates: they can be too small to justify the expense of employing a separate person to lead the caring system, but at the same time too large to permit the head of the institution to remain closely in touch with each inmate and staff member.

Our argument is, therefore, that change, though difficult, is possible. Much hinges on making more effective use of staff resources. In the next two sections we consider the problems of selecting and training staff and using their capacities.

HEADS OF INSTITUTIONS

We have already sufficiently underlined the importance of this role and the need for personal maturity in those who occupy it. We have also noted the relatively high turnover of people in this position.

It is a job for which there is no specific training or career path. Few of the heads we met had previous experience in this type of residential unit. Three kinds of background could be identified. Matrons and sisters-in-charge were always nurses, who had of course been trained in hospitals and often worked in them for extended periods. A second category included men and women with a history of residential work in other contexts, sometimes based on a social work qualification. The third came from outside the 'helping professions' altogether – for example, retired officers from the forces or former colonial officials.

Members of this last category perhaps have the least 'un-learning' to do, in that their previous experience is less apparently relevant. Because they are not identified with a professional caring role, they draw upon other skills which, if they relate to the management of activities and of groups of people, will be more appropriate to the institutional task than preoccupation with individual needs. When a trained nurse moves into a home for incurables, her basic activities seem the same but their context has subtly changed. She has to forgo the satisfactions that come from seeing her patients improve under her care. Instead of (as in the better hospitals) having total charge of a dependent patient for a relatively limited period of days or weeks, after which he is discharged and becomes independent of her, she has to learn to meet the dependent needs of a person who is (in the better institutions) concurrently finding satisfaction for his independent needs in other relationships and activities. Among heads of institutions who have previous experience of other kinds of residential care, those from old people's homes may underestimate inmates' capacities and needs for independence, whereas those from rehabilitative settings may overestimate them.

Turnover of heads of these institutions is almost certainly related to the stress of residential work with the disabled. Those who leave either move out of residential care altogether or transfer to other types of institution. It is a job which, especially in the larger units, requires demonstrable managerial capacities; yet there is practically no scope for promotion within the field. This points to a recruitment strategy which does not assume that one will discover the rare person who will prove both able and willing to dedicate his working life to the job; it may be more appropriate for the institution itself to set a limit to the period of employment. One possible device is to take in senior staff on secondment from other fields in which they have a permanent career – for example, the prison service or even industry. Another possibility is to look for an older person for whom this would be a terminal job. This last alternative is not without difficulties; but provided one ensures that the candidate already has a successful career behind him (and the accompanying security and confidence) and that he is seeking work rather than a sinecure, it is a solution that can be effective.

At present, no specific training is available for heads of this kind of institution and hardly any of those we met had attended

courses relevant to institutional management. Each one has to
formulate his own conception of residential care and to use
whatever experience and skills he has acquired elsewhere to
deal with the problems that arise. Two types of training would
be particularly appropriate for this situation. Group relations
training conferences (described in Rice, 1965) provide opportunities to learn at first hand about the nature of authority and
the interpersonal and intergroup problems encountered in
exercising it. These conferences, which are intended for people
in any leadership position, concentrate attention on the un-
conscious elements at work in group processes. The second
type of training, not at present available, would be specifically
aimed at helping heads of institutions to tease out the nature
and implications of their task and to find more effective ways
of carrying it out. During 1966-67, as an adjunct to our study,
we ran an experimental series of weekly seminars along these
lines. As might be expected, dependency was a constant underlying theme in these sessions: the pressures the group members
applied to us to provide them with solutions to insoluble
problems were plainly analogous to the pressures they themselves received from their own staff and inmates. Our refusal
to give answers that we had not got probably contributed to
the substantial drop-out of membership that occurred. Those
who stayed the course found some direct usefulness in comparing
their different approaches to common issues; but the greatest
benefit seemed to come from their recognition that the insoluble
problems were not a reflection of their own inadequacies and
they valued the sense of support that the group gave them. To
this extent the group was less concerned with training in the
conventional sense than with providing sanction for a certain
model of the leadership role – a function that would be particularly important if a number of institutions began to experiment with the approach to residential care that we have
delineated.[1]

---

[1] Our experimental seminar was based on the model of group training for general
practitioners which has been in use at the Tavistock Clinic, the Cassell Hospital,
and elsewhere for many years: see, for example, Balint (1964), Balint *et al.* (1966),
and Gosling *et al.* (1967).

OTHER STAFF

RHB units contain a high proportion of qualified nurses and most institutions employ at least one state registered nurse. Other types of qualification are rare. Training programmes in residential care are being started as a result of the recommendations of the Williams Report (National Council of Social Service, 1967), and at least one voluntary organization – the Cheshire Foundation – has been recruiting young people into a Service Corps, in which they receive a programme of training and practical experience before being assigned to jobs in the institutions. It will be a long time, however, before these schemes significantly increase the numbers of trained workers, and institutions will continue to be heavily reliant on unqualified staff as attendants.

Although there may be real difficulties in recruiting staff, some institutions themselves seem to place obstacles in the way of recruitment. For example, in one modern purpose-built establishment, the rooms for resident staff were inferior to those provided for inmates and thus attractive only to staff of inferior quality. The desirability of having staff living on the premises needs to be questioned in any case. Institutions that have the misfortune to be sited in remote areas cannot avoid supplying some accommodation; those in towns can be run entirely by non-resident staff, and there are many advantages in this. As with heads of institutions, it is desirable that the lives of other staff do not entirely revolve round the institution: they can work more effectively if they have other roles and other commitments outside in the local community. Some establishments deprive themselves of potential help by insisting that staff should be resident or at least work a full week; whereas there are many married women prepared to work for shorter spells. Voluntary workers too can be – and in some institutions are – used fruitfully, not only behind the scenes (for example, for laundry and mending linen), but to provide personal services to inmates (which can include letter-writing, hair-setting, feeding, washing, and bathing). The inconvenience of administering larger numbers of part-time staff, some paid and some honorary, is amply repaid in terms of the variety of relationships made available to inmates. The reality is that the number of people who are both willing and suitable to commit themselves to full-time permanent employment in these institutions is very small. More extended use of part-time staff or of staff on short-term contracts – for example, young people wanting to do a year's voluntary service – would both get the necessary chores done and relate the institution more effectively to the wider society.

For many of the jobs, the training is minimal. Much more important is the orientation of staff. The behavioural model set by the head of the institution and by the person in charge of the caring system is critical: this can either support or inhibit healthy dependency relationships. Stresses will nevertheless occur, and there is a need for the staff who provide physical care in particular to get away from inmates at times and to meet together as a group. Such meetings can be usefully structured to discuss various aspects of the work.

The head of the institution will be able to sustain more mature supportive roles in the group if he himself is supported through external relationships. In the training we have suggested, he would derive support from meeting others in similar positions; but his relationship with his own Management Committee may often have a critical effect.

MANAGEMENT COMMITTEES

In the voluntary sector, the Management Committee is often in close touch with the institution for which it is responsible and its members may be frequent visitors. If the visits are too frequent, staff may complain that they are not trusted to do their job; and a more subtle danger is that staff may become unrealistically dependent and encourage the outsiders to take decisions that staff are in a better position to take themselves. If the visits are not frequent enough, inmates may feel that they are being left at the mercy of less than adequate staff. Committee members usually find it extraordinarily difficult to evaluate the complaints they receive and to make realistic judgements about the way in which the institution as a whole is being run. In the case of RHB and local authority units, where the corresponding committee has wider responsibilities and is more remote, this problem of assessment is compounded. It is all too likely that visits will become formal occasions when both staff and inmates are on their best behaviour.

While lay people serving on these committees can scarcely be expected to be experts on physical disability and its attendant problems, good intentions (even if they are accompanied by deep purses) are not enough. Some of the difficulties over making assessments arise from the lack of a clear definition of the institution's task. If the committee shares such a definition with the head of the institution, it is in a much stronger position both to support him in implementing it and to develop criteria for task performance. In so far as a relatively high turnover of staff at all levels is predictable and even planned, the role of the Management Committee in maintaining the continuity of a particular philosophy of residential care will reduce the insecurity of the long-stay inmates.

In taking this role, the committee may benefit from advice from specialists outside the institution for which it is responsible. This and other possibilities are discussed in the next chapter. But (if we may return to a point made earlier in this chapter) the absence of expert advice can, in the pervasive dependent culture of residential care, too readily become another alibi for failing to attempt change. More money, better staff, more training, more enlightened public attitudes – all of these would indeed make it easier to institute change. Equally, one might say that if only the inmates were less crippled, physically and psychologically, the institutions would be better places to live in. If inmates are to be helped both to accept the realities of their dependence and to find roles through which to express their capacities for independence, Management Committees and heads of institutions have to use their leadership to set an example by accepting the real constraints, and only the real ones, under which they have to operate, and by displaying that they have the courage to experiment with changes and the determination to make them work.

CHAPTER 13

The Future

THE ROLE OF GOVERNMENT

Over the years the Department of Health and Social Security (which incorporates the former Ministry of Health) has set progressively higher standards for the residential care provided both through Regional Hospital Boards and through local authorities and voluntary bodies. For example, it has urged RHBs to get the younger chronic sick out of geriatric wards, encouraged the establishment of special units, and advised on standards of accommodation and physical amenities. While it has not pioneered new approaches, it has helped to ensure that the practices of the better institutions become models for the rest. Sponsorship of research such as our own is an aspect of the standard-setting process. So far, however, the advice given in the Department's circulars has been predominantly concerned with improvements in the physical environment. We believe that it should now become much more preoccupied with the psychosocial environment. The Department might, for example, endorse a definition of the primary task of these institutions along the lines we have suggested. Governmental leadership of this kind would provide valuable support and leverage for those local committees and heads of institutions who are willing to try innovations, and would perhaps give some stimulus to those who are still clinging to custodial values.

One possible objection is that in calling for opportunities for independence and choice as well as for the satisfaction of dependent needs, the government would be moving beyond the conventional goals of the health, welfare, and even educational services into the realms of personal development and quality of life. On the other hand, this is consistent with current social trends. There are many indications that the concept of the

220

welfare state, which itself is primarily concerned with satisfying dependent needs, is coming to be regarded as inadequate, and there are mounting demands, explicit and tacit, for greater opportunities for personal growth and self-expression. Social changes may therefore provide support for the changes we are advocating. But the sanction of an explicit government policy that reflects these changes remains desirable.

The need for more effective coordination of policy and practice at both national and local levels is now increasingly recognized. At present it is too often the vagaries of referral processes rather than the needs of the individual that determine whether he comes within the province of local authority services or the National Health Service. In some voluntary homes, people whose disabilities and needs for attention are similar are nevertheless paid for at different rates according to the source of referral. As the then Minister of Health, Kenneth Robinson, wrote in his foreword to the first Green Paper on the health services in 1968:

'The paramount requirement is that all the different kinds of care and treatment that an individual may need at different times, whether separately or in combination, should be readily available to him' (Ministry of Health, 1968b, p. 5).

The way in which administrative and professional boundaries are currently drawn is not always consistent with that requirement. However, at the time this chapter is being completed (early 1970) there are prospects of fairly radical reorganization. A second Green Paper on the National Health Service has just been published (Department of Health and Social Security, 1970). Its proposals for a new area organization are to some extent linked with the recommendations of the Maud Report (Royal Commission on Local Government, 1969) on local government. And although implementation of the Seebohm Report (Committee on Local Authority and Allied Personal Social Services, 1968) is still partly in doubt, the Local Authority Social Services Bill, which is now before Parliament, will require each local authority to establish a single committee and appoint a director to take responsibility for all social services.

Implications and Conclusions

The organizational changes that will emerge from these measures are likely to have at least as much effect on residential institutions as the more directly relevant Chronically Sick and Disabled Persons Bill, which is also currently being debated and which is intended to raise the standards of local services for the disabled to the level of the best existing practices. Although this is a private member's bill, it is going forward with government support.

ADMINISTRATIVE BOUNDARIES

An area organization in which the boundaries of health authorities and local authorities coincide should have many advantages. In particular, it should become more possible to design and implement integrated strategies of domiciliary and community care on the one hand and the use of residential institutions on the other.

At present, most of those for whom institutional care is sought are middle-aged or older. The younger disabled, for whom many institutions have aimed to cater, try to remain with their families as long as they can. Improved domiciliary services will foster this trend. The six-weeks-in, six-weeks-out policy adopted by some hospitals may well be extended; though this seems appropriate only as a transitional arrangement, not as a quasi-permanent strategy of care. Another factor that will affect requirements for institutional accommodation is the increasing emphasis on community care. Local authorities are experimenting in a modest way by providing purpose-built or specially adapted flats or bungalows for the disabled. As a result, a minority who would have entered, or actually had entered, residential institutions in the past have been able to make their lives outside. The increasing sophistication of electronic and other aids will also diminish dependence.

These trends are partly based on a wish to keep the crippled and elderly out of institutions. For example, Peter Townsend's argument (Townsend, 1968) for less investment in residential care and more in domiciliary services is based on the widespread and all too realistic belief that institutional life is a

222

living death. However well they are run, institutions for these categories of people are places where they go in order, sooner or later, to die and they have to cope with all the attendant problems. We have suggested, however, that an institution which sets out to become a good place to die in is likely to be a better place to live in, and that processes of institutionalization, though insidious, are not inevitable and irreversible. The appropriate policy, therefore, is not to cut down investment in residential facilities but to ensure that the investment produces better institutions. In this way, some cripples could be given a meaningful choice. Even now there are a few institutions in which inmates find a richer environment than at home.

The first Green Paper stated that 'the authorities of the future should have wide scope to bring together the related services and plan boldly for new patterns of care' (para. 18), and its successor expresses similar sentiments. Each authority will be catering for a sufficiently large disabled population to justify the creation of differentiated and specialized services which, we would hope, will go beyond standard-setting and inspection. They could have a significant role in staff training, for example, and in providing consultative services. In a memorandum to the Cheshire Foundation, we identified the need for two types of specialist service which could be appropriately set up for the Foundation's homes. We described the first as broadly an 'engineering' function, concerned with diminishing physical handicap, both by providing prosthetic aids for the individual and by modifying his physical environment in ways that would bring it more fully under his control. The second would be concerned with ameliorating the psychosocial environment. There would be room for both types of expertise in the area authority.

Moreover, it should be possible at area level to reinforce the support activities which, as we pointed out in Chapter 11, though necessary to the task of the institution, may be beyond its resources to sustain as a differentiated function. For example, a peripatetic social worker might serve several establishments. This is also a function to which local clergy could make a valid contribution if trained to do so. The authority should be able to provide training and support not only for clergy but for all the voluntary workers involved with the disabled.

The authority will have a substantial budget at its disposal and can use this to foster the better kinds of care. It is our impression that voluntary homes actually or potentially provide the best milieux. Hospitals, whether voluntary or under NHS auspices, are inevitably dominated by the medical structure and culture. This extends even to the few specialized units where inmates are allowed to have personal possessions and a little privacy. Under a medical and nursing régime the inmate is inevitably defined as a patient, and care is geared to the most helpless. Moreover, in addition to the problem of a dependent culture, the split between the medical, nursing, and administrative hierarchies means that the person in charge of a health service unit — most probably a matron — is unable to exercise the authority that the head of an institution needs to have. When we add to these points the fact that the cost per patient per week is much higher in RHB units than in voluntary homes that accept RHB patients, there is clearly a case for re-examining policy. It is true that RHB contributions for inmates in voluntary homes often fall short of covering running expenses, while capital costs are borne entirely from voluntary sources; but even if the full costs proved to be equal, it would be prudent to subsidize more places in voluntary homes, which do not suffer from the built-in disadvantages of the hospital culture. Hospital units would then be appropriately reserved for irretrievably dependent long-term cases, such as brain-damaged paraplegics. Programmes of domiciliary and community care will doubtless gradually increase the proportion of such cases in residential units, but so long as the individual going into residential care is potentially capable of taking up independent roles, however limited, he should be admitted to an institution that can provide them.

PROFESSIONAL BOUNDARIES

One advantage of the voluntary home is that it is able to evade a spurious either/or distinction: either the individual needs medical and nursing attention and goes into a hospital unit;

or he does not, and becomes a charge on the local authority's welfare department. In the voluntary home, treatment and welfare can coexist. But both treatment and welfare imply a dependent relationship and the institutional task goes beyond this: provision for independent roles is also required.

Although the caring system is largely engaged in helping inmates with daily living activities, the fact remains that for many of them minor colds and coughs can lead to major complications. Many, too, require regular injections and other treatments that need supervision. It is, therefore, doubtful whether the leadership of the caring system could be in the hands of anyone but a trained nurse. However, because the hospital culture in which nurses have been trained is in some respects at odds with the institutional task, we have expressed reservations about employing nurses as heads of institutions; if they are to do their job, they have to move away from the culture in which they have been trained and which supports them through the stresses of their role.

Social work is in some respects a more suitable background than nursing. Whereas the nurse normally has her patient only in the dependent relationship – when he gets better she will not see him again – the social worker is trying to strengthen the client's capacities for independence and progressively reduce the dependency. But both professions are basically concerned with cure and rehabilitation, so that, if they are to take appropriate staff roles in these institutions, social workers, like nurses, have to relinquish some of the values inherent in their training.

The Williams Report recommends establishing a form of training specific to residential homes and providing a career structure for their staff. In effect, it proposes to make residential care a profession. As we implied in the last chapter, we have hesitations about this solution. First, we doubt whether there are more than a few people who are both willing and suitable to make a career in residential institutions for incurables. Second, we believe that the task and problems of these institutions are so radically different from those of institutions concerned with development and rehabilitation that they cannot appropriately be lumped together.

Implications and Conclusions

Essentially we are saying that the way in which professional boundaries have been and are being drawn is inconsistent with the needs of cripples in institutions. Cripples do not adequately fit the role of patient or client; and as inmates they differ on the one hand from young people in children's homes and approved schools and on the other hand from the aged residents of old people's homes. The fact that they do not fit any of these accepted roles almost certainly adds to their deprivation; yet they are too few to justify a profession that will make them its sole concern.

However, if one adds to the numbers actually in residential care the many other cripples who are currently being supported in the community but will eventually need it, this constraint is removed. In other words, there might be a nucleus of professionals whose job straddled both residential care and domiciliary support. Such mobility across the institutional boundary, combined perhaps with greater facility for the potential inmate himself to move in and out several times before final admission, could make the institution less oppressive for both parties. There will certainly be an opportunity for area health authorities to experiment jointly with local authority services along these lines.

In one sense, what we are suggesting here is a supplement or substitute for the declining religious institutions which have in the past had the social function of helping people to deal with their problems of mortality and bereavement. Like other suggestions in this book, however, it can be no panacea. Individuals will continue to experience the physical and emotional pain of becoming irretrievably crippled, ageing, deteriorating, and dying; and many will continue to spend much of their lives in institutions. But perhaps they can be given slightly more effective support during these processes.

References

ALLEN, F. H. & PEARSON, G. H. J. (1928). The emotional problems of the physically handicapped child. *Journal of Medical Psychology* **8**, pp. 212-35.

BALINT, M. (1964). *The doctor, his patient and the illness*. Second edn. London: Pitman; New York: International Universities Press.

BALINT, M., BALINT, E., GOSLING, R. & HILDEBRAND, P. (1966). *A study of doctors*. London: Tavistock; Philadelphia: Lippincott.

BANNISTER, K. *et al.* (1955). *Social casework in marital problems: the development of a psychodynamic approach*. London: Tavistock.

BANNISTER, K. & PINCUS, L. (1965). *Shared phantasy in marital problems: therapy in a four-person relationship*. Hitchin, Herts.: Codicote Press.

BARKER, R. G. (1948). The social psychology of physical disability. *Journal of Social Issues* **4**, pp. 28-38.

BARKER, R. G., WRIGHT, B. & GONICK, M. R. (1946). Adjustment to physical handicap and illness: a survey of the social psychology of physique and disability. New York: *Social Science Research Council Bulletin* 55.

BARTON, R. (1966). *Institutional neurosis*. Second edition. Bristol: Wright.

BATTYE, L. (1966). The Chatterley syndrome. In Hunt (1966), pp. 3-16.

BELKNAP, I. (1956). *Human problems of a state mental hospital*. New York: McGraw-Hill.

BEN-DAVID, J. (1958). The professional role of the physician in bureaucratized medicine: a study in role conflict. *Human Relations* **11**, pp. 255-74.

BION, W. R. (1961). *Experiences in groups*. London: Tavistock. Social Science Paperback, 1968.

BOWLBY, J. (1953). *Child care and the growth of love*. Harmondsworth: Penguin Books.

BOWLBY, J., ROBERTSON, J. & ROSENBLUTH, D. (1952). A two-year-old goes to hospital. *Psychoanalytic Study of the Child* **7**, pp. 82-94.

BOYLE, A. (1955). *No passing glory*. London: Collins.

BRADDON, R. (1954). *Cheshire, V.C.* London: Evans.

References

BRIDGER, H. (1946). The Northfield experiment. *Bulletin of the Menninger Clinic* **10** (3), pp. 71-6.

BRIDGER, H., MILLER, E. J. & O'DWYER, J. J. (1964). The doctor and sister in industry: a study of change. (Reprinted from *Occupational Health*, 1963.) London: Macmillan (Journals) Ltd.

BROWN, H. (1966). Some anomalies of social welfare. In Hunt (1966), pp. 133-41.

BURLINGHAM, D. (1965). Some problems of ego development in blind children. *Psychoanalytic Study of the Child* **20**, pp. 194-208.

CARLING, F. (1962). *And yet we are human*. London: Chatto & Windus.

CAUDILL, W. A. (1958). *The psychiatric hospital as a small society*. Cambridge, Mass.: Harvard University Press.

CENTERS, L. & R. (1963). Peer group attitudes towards the amputee child. *Journal of Social Psychology* **61**, pp. 127-32.

COMFORT, A. (1967). Institutions without sex. *New Society* **9** (223), 5 January, p. 5.

COMMITTEE ON LOCAL AUTHORITY AND ALLIED PERSONAL SOCIAL SERVICES (1968). *Report* (the Seebohm Report). London: HMSO (Cmnd. 3703).

COSER, L. A. (1967). Greedy organisations. *Arch. Europ. de Sociologie* **8** (2), pp. 196-215.

DEPARTMENT OF HEALTH AND SOCIAL SECURITY (1970). *National health service: the future structure of the national health service*. London: HMSO.

DICKS, H. V. (1967). *Marital tensions: clinical studies towards a psychological theory of interaction*. London: Routledge & Kegan Paul.

DINITZ, S. *et al.* (1958). The ward behaviour of psychiatric patients. *Social Problems* **6**, pp. 107-15.

EMERY, F. E. & TRIST, E. L. (1960). Socio-technical systems. In C. W. Churchman & M. Verhulst (eds.), *Management sciences*. Oxford: Pergamon.

FARNDALE, J. (ed.) (1965). *Trends in social welfare*. Oxford/New York: Pergamon Press.

FIELD, M. (1953). *Patients are people*. New York: Columbia University Press.

FRAZER, Sir J. G. (1935). *The scapegoat*. New York: Macmillan.

GOFFMAN, E. (1958). The characteristics of total institutions. Symposium on preventive and social psychiatry, Washington.

GOFFMAN, E. (1961). *Asylums: essays on the social situation of mental patients and other inmates*. New York: Doubleday Anchor Books.

GOFFMAN, E. (1963). *Stigma: notes on the management of spoiled identity.* Englewood Cliffs, N.J.: Prentice-Hall; Harmondsworth: Penguin Books, 1968.

GOLDSMITH, S. (1966). A home for the disabled: Bishop Herbert House, Norwich. *The Architects' Journal Information Library,* pp. 993-1004.

GOLDSMITH, S. (1967). *Designing for the disabled.* Second edition. London: Royal Institute of British Architects.

GORER, G. (1965). *Death, grief and mourning in contemporary Britain.* London: Cresset Press.

GOSLING, R., MILLER, D., TURQUET, P. M. & WOODHOUSE, D. L. (1967). *The use of small groups in training.* London: Tavistock Institute of Medical Psychology. Hitchin, Herts.: Codicote Press.

GREENBLATT, M., LEVINSON, D. J. & WILLIAMS, R. H. (eds.) (1957). *The patient and the mental hospital.* Glencoe, Ill.: The Free Press.

HANKS, J. R. & HANKS, L. M. Jr. (1948). The physically handicapped in certain non-occidental societies. *Journal of Social Issues* **4,** pp. 11-20.

HENRICH, E. & KRIEGEL, L. (eds.) (1961). *Experiments in survival.* New York: Association for the Aid of Crippled Children.

HIGGINS, R. (1963). Permanence in institutions. *New Society* **2** (41), 11 July, pp. 9-11.

HUNT, P. (ed.) (1966). *Stigma: the experience of disability.* London: Geoffrey Chapman.

JANOWITZ, M. (1966). Foreword to Street, Vinter & Perrow (1966).

JAQUES, E. (1951). *The changing culture of a factory.* London: Tavistock/Routledge.

JAQUES, E. (1955). Social systems as a defence against persecutory and depressive anxiety. In M. Klein, P. Heimann & R. E. Money-Kyrle (eds.), *New directions in psycho-analysis.* London: Tavistock.

JAQUES, E. (1956). *Measurement of responsibility: a study of work, payment and individual capacity.* London: Tavistock.

JAQUES, E. (1961). *Equitable payment: a general theory of work, differential payment, and individual progress.* London: Heinemann.

JONES, M. *et al.* (1952). *Social psychiatry: a study of therapeutic communities.* London: Tavistock/Routledge. Published in the USA as *The therapeutic community.* New York: Basic Books, 1953.

JULES, H. (1957). Types of institutional structure. *Psychiatry* **20,** pp. 47-60.

KAHN, R. L. *et al.* (1964). *Organizational stress: studies in role conflict and ambiguity.* New York: Wiley.

References

KAPLAN, E. B. (1965). Reflections regarding psychomotor activities during the latency period. *Psychoanalytic Study of the Child* **20**, pp. 220-37.

KLECK, R. (1969). Physical stigma and task oriented interactions. *Human Relations* **22** (1), pp. 53-60.

KLECK, R., ONO, H. & HASTORF, A. H. (1966). The effects of physical deviance upon face-to-face interaction. *Human Relations* **19** (4), pp. 425-36.

KLEIN, M. (1959). Our adult world and its roots in infancy. *Human Relations* **12**, pp. 291-303. Reprinted in M. Klein, *Our adult world and other essays*. London: Heinemann, 1963.

LOEWENSTEIN, R. M. (1950). Conflict and autonomous ego development during the phallic phase. *Psychoanalytic Study of the Child* **5**, pp. 47-52.

LUSSIER, A. (1960). The analysis of a boy with a congenital deformity. *Psychoanalytic Study of the Child* **15**, pp. 430-53.

MAIN, T. F. (1946). The hospital as a therapeutic institution. *Bulletin of the Menninger Clinic* **10** (3), pp. 66-70.

MARTIN, D. V. (1962). *Adventure in psychiatry: social change in a mental hospital*. Oxford: Bruno Cassirer.

MENG, H. (1938). Zur Socialpsychologie der Korperbeschadigten: ein Beitrag zum Problem der praktischen Psychohygiene. *Schweizer Archiv für Neurologie und Psychiatrie* **40**, pp. 328-44.

MENZIES, I. E. P. (1960). A case-study in the functioning of social systems as a defence against anxiety. *Human Relations* **13**, pp. 95-121. Reprinted (pamphlet) by Tavistock Institute of Human Relations, London, 1970.

MEYERSON, L. (1948a). Physical disability as a social psychological problem. *Journal of Social Issues* **4** (4), pp. 2-20.

MEYERSON, L. (1948b). Experimental injury: an approach to the dynamics of disability. *Journal of Social Issues* **4** (4), pp. 68-71.

MILLER, E. J. (1959). Technology, territory and time: the internal differentiation of complex production systems. *Human Relations* **12**, pp. 243-72.

MILLER, E. J. & RICE, A. K. (1967). *Systems of organization*. London: Tavistock.

MINISTRY OF HEALTH (1968a). Care of younger chronic sick patients in hospitals. Circular HM(68)41.

MINISTRY OF HEALTH (1968b). *National health service: the administrative structure of the medical and related services in England and Wales*. London: HMSO.

MITTELMAN, B. (1960). Intrauterine and early infantile motility. *Psychoanalytic Study of the Child* **15**, pp. 104-27.

MUSSEN, P. H. & BARKER, R. G. (1944). Attitudes towards cripples. *Journal of Abnormal and Social Psychology* **39**.

NATIONAL COUNCIL OF SOCIAL SERVICE (1958). *Help for the handicapped*. An enquiry into the opportunities of the voluntary services. Ditchling Press.

NATIONAL COUNCIL OF SOCIAL SERVICE (1967). *Caring for people: staffing residential homes*. The report of the committee of enquiry set up by the National Council of Social Service (the Williams Report). London: Allen & Unwin.

NIEDERLAND, W. G. (1965). Narcissistic ego impairment in patients with early physical malformations. *Psychoanalytic Study of the Child* **20**, pp. 518-34.

OSWIN, M. (1968). The empty hours. *Our Children*, Autumn, pp. 9-17. (Council for Children's Welfare, London.)

PINCUS, L. (ed.) (1960). *Marriage: studies in emotional conflict and growth*. London: Methuen.

PROSEN, H. (1965). Physical disability and motivation. *Canadian Medical Association Journal* **92**, 12 June, pp. 1261-5.

RAPOPORT, R. N. (1960). *Community as doctor: new perspectives on a therapeutic community*. London: Tavistock. Social Science Paperback, 1967.

RICE, A. K. (1958). *Productivity and social organization: the Ahmedabad experiment*. London: Tavistock. Social Science Paperback, 1970.

RICE, A. K. (1963). *The enterprise and its environment*. London: Tavistock. Social Science Paperback, 1971.

RICE, A. K. (1965). *Learning for leadership*. London: Tavistock. Social Science Paperback, 1971.

RICE, A. K. & TRIST, E. L. (1952). Institutional and sub-institutional determinants of change in labour turnover. *Human Relations* **5**, pp. 347-71.

RICHARDSON, S. A. (1963). Some social psychological consequences of handicapping. *Pediatrics* **32**, pp. 291-7.

ROBB, B. (1967). *Sans everything: a case to answer*. London: Nelson.

ROYAL COMMISSION ON LOCAL GOVERNMENT IN ENGLAND, 1966-1969 (1969). *Report*, Vol. 1 (the Maud Report). London: HMSO (Cmnd. 4040).

SCHILDER, P. (1950). *The image and appearance of the human body*. New York: International Universities Press.

SOFER, C. (1961). *The organization from within*. London: Tavistock.

STANTON, A. H. (1956). The study of the psychiatric hospital as a therapeutic society. *Centennial Papers*, St Elizabeth's Hospital, Washington, D.C.

References

STANTON, A. H. & SCHWARTZ, M. S. (1949). The management of a type of institutional participation in mental illness. *Psychiatry* **12**, pp. 13-26.

STANTON, A. H. & SCHWARTZ, M. S. (1954). *The mental hospital.* New York: Basic Books.

STREET, D., VINTER, R. D. & PERROW, C. (1966). *Organization for treatment: a comparative study of institutions for delinquents.* New York: The Free Press. London: Collier-Macmillan.

TOWNSEND, P. (1962). *The last refuge: a survey of residential institutions and homes for the aged in England and Wales.* London: Routledge & Kegan Paul.

TOWNSEND, P. (1967). *The disabled in society.* Lecture read at the Royal College of Surgeons.

TOWNSEND, P. (1968). Family welfare and Seebohm. *New Society* **12** (305), 1 August, pp. 159-60.

TRIST, E. L. & BAMFORTH, K. W. (1951). Some social and psychological consequences of the longwall method of coal-getting. *Human Relations* **4**, pp. 3-38.

TRIST, E. L., HIGGIN, G. W., MURRAY, H. A. & POLLOCK, A. B. (1963). *Organizational choice: capabilities of groups at the coal face under changing technologies.* London: Tavistock.

VON HENTIG, H. (1948). Physical disability, mental conflict and social crisis. *Journal of Social Issues* **4**, pp. 21-7.

WALLACE, A. C. & RASHKIS, H. A. (1963). The relation of staff consensus to patient disturbance on mental hospital wards. Pp. 630-6 in N. J. & W. T. Smelser (eds.), *Personality and social system.* New York: Wiley.

WHITEMAN, M. & LUKOFF, I. F. (1964). Attitudes towards blindness in two college groups. *Journal of Social Psychology* **63**, pp. 179-91.

WHITEMAN, M. & LUKOFF, I. F. (1965). Attitudes towards blindness and other physical handicaps. *Journal of Social Psychology* **66**, pp. 135-45.

WING, J. K. (1962). Institutionalism in mental hospitals. *British Journal of Social and Clinical Psychology* **1**, p. 38.

WRIGHT, B. A. (1960). *Physical disability: a psychological approach.* New York: Harper.

Index

accommodation, for disabled, 44, 146, 222
achievement, 26
emphasis on, 139-41, 163, 195
action research, 5, 6, 21-2, 23, 24, 31
see also pilot study
admission, to residential institutions, 13, 199-200, 202-3
age-limits, 63-4, 96, 99, 100, 102, 103
applications, 94-5
experience of, 104-9
problems of rejection, 13, 103-4, 109, 200
procedures, 93-101
see also selection
age distribution of residents, *see* residents
age-structure of population, 57
aggressiveness, 51, 52, 54, 120
apathy, 20, 53, 104, 140, 143, 148, 150, 155, 192
area health authorities, 226
assessment holiday, 94-5, 96, 97, 101, 106, 107, 108, 206
autonomy, personal, 19, 26
see also independence

Barker, R. G., 44, 49
Barton, Russell, 3
Battye, L., 47-8

Belknap, I., 3
Ben-David, J., 168
Bion, W. R., 200-1
body image, distortion of, 52, 53

canonization, 89, 126, 184
capacities of disabled, *see* disabled
caring system, *see* dependence system
Carnegie United Kingdom Trust, 25
Caudill, W. A., 3
cerebral palsy, 56, 70
changing culture of a factory, The, 17
Cheshire, Group Captain Leonard, 24, 27, 30, 57
Cheshire Foundation, 25, 29, 30-1, 34, 37, 223
Service Corps training school, 30, 217
Cheshire homes, 16, 24, 30-1, 186
see also Le Court
Cheshire Smile, The, 16
choice, exercise of, 89, 104-8, 142-3, 145, 148, 153, 161, 172, 213, 220
see also conflict
Chronically Sick and Disabled Persons Bill, 222

233